The
MAKING
of a
CHAMPION

The
MAKING
of a
CHAMPION

Lester Sumrall

Whitaker House

THE MAKING OF A CHAMPION

Lester Sumrall
Lester Sumrall Evangelistic Association, Inc.
P.O. Box 12
South Bend, IN 46624

ISBN: 0-88368-366-0
Printed in the United States of America
Copyright © 1995 by Whitaker House

Whitaker House
580 Pittsburgh Street
Springdale, PA 15144

Contents

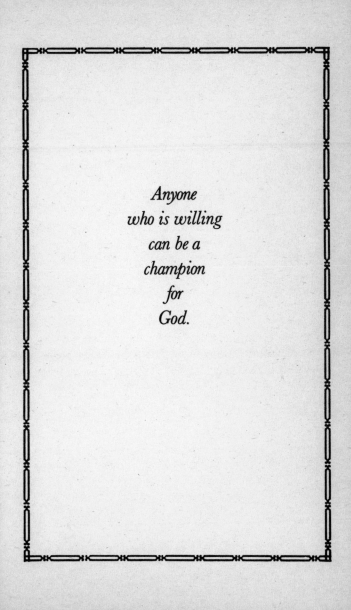

*Anyone
who is willing
can be a
champion
for
God.*

1

You Can Be a Champion

While in Jerusalem recently, I had an opportunity to preach in the shadow of the great stone walls of the ancient city. Standing there, I could not help thinking of Nehemiah, the man who once rebuilt those walls. Coming out of captivity in a foreign land, he united and led a rag-tag group of workers to build those walls in a very short time and against incredible odds.

What a champion he was! As I studied the great stones, I was overwhelmed by the magnitude of the task Nehemiah took on himself. This was no small chore. The wall itself is massive, a marvel of design and engineering. Nehemiah had no power tools, cranes, or heavy machinery to lift the giant stones into place. The task he accomplished in a few weeks' time is one of the wonders of ancient construction.

More than that, Nehemiah labored amid vicious opposition. His enemies were relentless. They tried every conceivable tactic to impede Nehemiah's great work. Yet Nehemiah faithfully kept at it until his task was complete.

A Book for All of Us

Nehemiah's story is usually viewed as a study in leadership, and that's one way to look at it. His problems were the classic problems that all leaders face. His methods were the methods of wise leadership. And his triumph was a triumph of great leadership.

Let me remind you, however, that Nehemiah did not begin his work as a leader in the normal sense. He was not a Levite—a member of Israel's priestly tribe—or a ruler of anything. He was a servant, a layman—just an individual with a heart for God. In that sense, he is a great example to the people of God for all time. He is a lesson to us that God uses the weak things of the world to accomplish His work (cf. 1 Cor. 1:26–31). Position and title are unimportant. No matter who you are, *you* can be a champion for God.

Thus, more than a textbook on leadership, the book of Nehemiah is a manual for the layperson, the man or woman of God who wants to live a life that counts. Nehemiah teaches us that whoever we are, whatever our position in life, we can be true champions who make a real difference in our society.

Familiar Circumstances

Nehemiah came on the scene in Israel almost a century after the first Jews had returned to the Promised Land from the Babylonian captivity. Zerubbabel, the great and godly leader who had brought that first wave of captives back to Jerusalem, was dead. Ezra, who had led a second wave of people back, was apparently gone from the scene for the time being. The people were devoid of spiritual direction when Nehemiah stepped up and challenged them to help him rebuild the walls.

The day I preached in the shadow of those great walls, two and a half millennia after Nehemiah struggled to build them, I was struck by the similarities between our time and his. The Israelites are returning to the Promised Land again. The walls, scarred by years of abuse and neglect, are once again in need of repair. They stand as a mute testimony that time may crumble brick and mortar, but it does not alter the human experience.

Just as in Nehemiah's day, there is a great lack of spiritual direction. The desperate need is for someone who will step forward with a challenge—a champion ready to lead God's people in rebuilding the walls that have crumbled.

I'm not talking now about national Israel or the literal walls around Jerusalem. The spiritual aimlessness that threatens modern man is a world-wide phenomenon. It touches every civilization and society at almost every level. And the walls that so urgently need to be rebuilt are the walls of righteousness, morality, and holiness unto the Lord—the protective walls that are essential to the survival of humanity.

Where are the champions who will rebuild those walls, worn and decaying with time? Where are those who will rise to unite God's people and overcome the lethargy and division that threaten to leave all of civilization in ruins?

In Search of a Genuine Champion

The modern spiritual crisis is a two-pronged peril. Not only is there a shortage of true champions, but even more foreboding, contemporary society also seems to have completely forgotten what it is that qualifies a man or woman to stand up and speak for God. Modern culture is so preoccupied with the ideas of celebrity, popularity, and status that a real champion, if one came on the scene, would not be quickly recognized.

For decades, the heroes in our society have been entertainment figures, athletes, and other media creations who more often than not utterly lack character. Slowly but surely, this kind of thinking has even crept into the church. Unfortunately, many of today's "spiritual leaders" are cut from the same mold as the world's heroes. They're entertainers and celebrities, admired for their charm and good looks rather than because they live lives of holiness unto the Lord.

We're shocked—and rightly so—when a nationally known preacher admits to an adulterous affair. But that kind of scandal shouldn't really surprise us. When talent, prestige, popularity, glamour, personality, or anything other than blameless character become the criteria for spiritual leadership, an environment exists in which false champions will prosper. It's hard to keep up a front for long, and when the fragile facade crumbles, the devil has a heyday. Every time a so-called leader fails, it compounds the cynicism with which the world views the Lord's work. Never have true champions been more sorely needed than today.

What is it that makes a real champion? That's what we

hope to learn from the life of Nehemiah. But the starting point is to realize that the key to being a person God can use mightily is not fame, not intellect, not magnetism, not skill, not the ability to communicate, not wit, not human excellence, not stature, and not political acumen. It is *character*.

Nehemiah succeeded because he was a man of character. That's the long and the short of it. His secret was nothing mysterious—it was that he refused to compromise moral integrity, no matter what the cost to him personally. He never operated on the basis of expediency. He wasn't always diplomatic. He could hardly have been described as charming. He didn't fit any of our preconceptions about what a great leader might be. But that is exactly what made him a classic champion.

Think of those in Scripture who were true champions, and you'll note a definite pattern. They were used by God because of their character, not because of their stature. God started the nation of Israel through faithful Abraham, not through shrewd and selfish Lot. He used lowly David, not the imposing King Saul, to bring down the giant Goliath. Jesus called His disciples, bypassing the learned and intellectual religious leaders, choosing instead sincere men with hungry hearts.

They were like Nehemiah, who was like David, who was like Abraham. All were men of character. And they give us God's pattern for a truly great champion.

All the real men and women of God I have ever known fit this same pattern. They are used by God not because of their innate ability, but because of their faithfulness to Him. That's why I'm not afraid to step out in faith. I know success or failure in my ministry does not depend on my own skill or even on external circumstances; it depends only on my faithfulness. God will give me the gifts necessary to do whatever He calls me to do, and He will not be hindered in His work by circumstances.

Years ago, when I first sensed the call of God to preach, many people tried to dissuade me. My own father mocked me and told me I would starve to death. I overheard another close relative say that I would never be a preacher in a thousand years. Everyone seemed to think I would fail. Consequently, I began to wonder if they were right.

But you can't be a champion by retreating all the time, and I knew in my heart what God was calling me to do. I've never regretted stepping out in faith, either. God has supplied all my needs, and people have been more responsive to my ministry than I ever thought possible. My whole life is proof that what makes the most sense to human wisdom is not necessarily God's will.

I want to be a champion for God in my sphere of influence, and I hope that's the desire of your heart, too. As we look together at the making of a champion, Nehemiah will be our teacher. His lessons are easy to understand but difficult to apply. Study with me his life and the written legacy he left us. Drink in the simple truths he has to teach.

Above all, purpose to be a doer of the word, and not a hearer only. It will surely be painful to see our shortcomings in the light of Nehemiah's example. And it is certain to be costly to follow in his footsteps. The question is, are you willing to bear the pain and pay the price?

How you answer will ultimately determine whether you are a true champion or just another pretender.

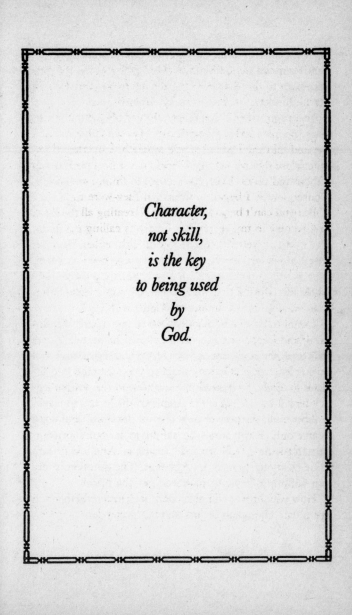

Character,
not skill,
is the key
to being used
by
God.

2

Be All You Can Be

*S*ome individuals seem born to greatness. No one really is.

Certainly, some people are born with incredible talent, marvelous athletic abilities, stunning artistic gifts, or other inherent aptitudes that make them stand head and shoulders above everyone else. But skill and natural giftedness do not equate with genuine greatness. They may magnify a person's greatness, but they are never the reason for it.

On the other hand, a truly great individual may be without exceptional talent, power, or fame. Real greatness grows out of character. A man or woman of character is a great person, whether or not others recognize it. A person of weak character is not great, no matter how much fame or worldly success comes along.

History is strewn with the litter of gifted individuals

who utterly failed when their character was tested. These people may be well known and influential in history—we even marvel at their extraordinary natural capabilities—but few would argue that they were truly great.

Aaron Burr is one such person. History gives him prominence, but only in the sense that it remembers him as a tragic failure. His life was a monument to squandered potential.

Burr's father and grandfather were godly men. His father, the Reverend Aaron Burr, was the second president of Princeton College. His grandfather, Jonathan Edwards, is best known for his fiery preaching. Edwards was used mightily of God during the Great Awakening in colonial America. He was also briefly President of Princeton, an office he held when he died.

Burr himself was brilliant. His academic record at Princeton has never been surpassed to this day. But his lusts were unquenchable, he lacked personal discipline, and his behavior often reflected immaturity. He joined the colonial army, but he got in a fight with General Washington and deserted his post. He was successful for a time in politics and even held the office of vice president of the United States. But he was suspected of tampering with votes to steal elections.

Burr shot and killed Alexander Hamilton in a duel, and then he fled to Europe to avoid prosecution. He eventually found his way back to New York, where he died friendless, penniless, and in disgrace. His great intellect and giftedness had brought him fame and position, but they could not make him a great man.

You don't have to go far back in history to find similar

examples. Think of the sports figures, show business celebrities, and business leaders in our generation who have
thrown away great potential and wound up as tragic figures. Their chief legacy is that they died of a drug over-
dose, committed some crime, or otherwise failed at
greatness, all because they lacked character.

An Ordinary Man . . .

Nehemiah was not that kind of man. He had no rich
heritage to lean on, no inherited fame or status to try to
live up to, no amazing physical strength or abilities to
show off. The sum of all biblical revelation about his back-
ground is contained in one brief phrase. It is only a portion of the first verse of the book that bears his name:
"Nehemiah the son of Hachaliah." That's all we know of
his ancestry. We don't know who his father, Hachaliah,
was; he's never mentioned in any other biblical genealogy.
He was probably from the tribe of Judah, but we don't
even know that for sure.

We can be reasonably certain, however, that if there
had been any great men or other champions in Nehemiah's bloodline, Scripture would have said so. Hebrew
genealogy had a way of recording and emphasizing such
significant details.

He was an ordinary man, bereft of any inherited quali-
ties that would put him in a place of prominence. He was
a servant, one man with no special training that would
qualify him for the great task to which God would call
him.

He was exactly the kind of person God delights to use.

. . . Extraordinary Character

There must have been lots of men more distinguished than Nehemiah both in Jerusalem and throughout the kingdom of Persia. Why did God use him to rebuild the city walls? Because Nehemiah was an ordinary man with extraordinary character.

The complete biblical account of Nehemiah's life and work reveals no blemish on his character. He exemplified piety, integrity, faithfulness, patriotism, diligence, humility, and a host of other virtues. He was a man of initiative. He had learned the language of his captors, and he worked hard and took advantage of every opportunity that came his way.

Nehemiah's zeal for the Lord set a high standard for everyone in Judah. That's all the more remarkable in light of the fact that he was not of the priestly caste. He was a simple layman. Though the laborer is worthy of his hire (see Luke 10:7), Nehemiah refused to accept compensation for his work (see Neh. 5:14–18), because he saw himself as working for the Lord. And he elevated the role of the layman to an unprecedented height.

Nehemiah was the consummate layman, but his type is an extremely rare bird. He was the kind of person every pastor hopes his church will be populated with, though the truth is that most of us would be happy with just one like him in the congregation.

Don't ever get the idea that serving the Lord as a layperson is less important than being a pastor or missionary. God calls and uses people in a lay capacity as surely as He uses people called "reverend" or "doctor." In fact, there are some tasks that can be done only by laypeople. Many individuals can be reached for Christ only by fellow workers on the job or friends in the neighborhood. They would never set foot in a church or talk to a pastor, and if they're going to hear the gospel, they'll have to hear it from a layperson. Thank God for the work He has accomplished over the years through laypeople!

Nehemiah, as a layman, was perfectly suited for his calling. He could approach the people of Jerusalem as one of their peers. Unlike the priests or scribes, Nehemiah could challenge the people from an equal footing. He could stand among them as a true fellow worker and lead them by example in a uniquely effective way.

A Bit of History

Nehemiah's ancestors had been forced from their homeland when Nebuchadnezzar invaded Judah in 586 B.C. It was an act of judgment on the Jewish nation orchestrated by God. Nebuchadnezzar's armies had ransacked and defiled the Temple, laid waste to Jerusalem, destroyed the walls that surrounded it, burned the gates, and marched the people off into captivity (see 2 Chron. 36:18–19).

That wall and those gates lay in ruins for more than a hundred years, a symbol of the broken Jewish nation. Psalm 137 records one of the popular songs of Nehemiah's time. It graphically describes the bitter experiences of the people under their barbaric foreign rulers:

> By the rivers of Babylon, there we sat down, yea, we wept when we remembered Zion. We hung our

harps upon the willows in the midst of it. For there those that carried us away captive required of us a song, and those who plundered us required of us mirth, saying, "Sing us one of the songs of Zion!" How shall we sing the LORD's song in a foreign land? (vv. 1–4)

And the bitterness the Jewish people felt toward their captors: "O daughter of Babylon, who are to be destroyed, happy shall he be who repays you as you have served us! Happy shall he be who takes and dashes your little ones against the rock" (vv. 8–9).

After more than a half-century of captivity to the Babylonians, the Jewish people found themselves under the rule of a new empire. The Persians defeated Babylon in 539 B.C., and Cyrus ascended the throne as king. He united Media and the Persian Empire into one great nation. In 538, in one of his first official acts as ruler of Babylon, he issued a decree that the Jews could return home.

About 42,000 Jews did return immediately, with Zerubbabel, Jeshua the high priest, and most of the sacred vessels of the Temple (see Ezra 1:11; 2:1–70). That should have been the beginning of a new era for the Hebrew nation. But the experience of those who returned was more like a broken record than a new start.

The rebuilding of the Temple was hampered by opposition from pagans who had settled in the land. Discouraged by the immensity of their task, the Jews stopped after the altar had been restored and the foundation laid. The Temple sat like that for sixteen years, until Haggai and

Zechariah stirred the conscience of the people. Then they finally finished the Temple, twenty years after they had returned to the land. The city walls and gates, however, still lay in ruins.

In 458 B.C., sixty years after the Temple was completed, a second wave of returnees, led by Ezra, entered Jerusalem. Still, only a small minority of the Jews in dispersion had returned. Most remained in foreign lands.

The Right Man in the Right Place at the Right Time

Nehemiah was one of those who had not returned. Generations of Nehemiah's family had stayed outside their homeland, living in servitude to the Persian Empire. By the time Nehemiah was born, the empire encompassed India, Greece, Europe, and Africa. The Persian capital was Shushan, or Susa, and that's where Nehemiah lived. It is probable that he had never seen Jerusalem before the Lord laid it on his heart to go there and rebuild the city's ruined walls.

When we first meet Nehemiah, it was about 445 B.C.— nearly a century after the decree of Cyrus had opened the way for Jews to return to their homeland. Nehemiah was in the Persian royal palace, serving as cupbearer to the king. He told about it in typically humble fashion, in the closing verse of the first chapter, almost incidentally: "For I was the king's cupbearer" (1:11).

It wasn't a bad job. His access to the king during private mealtimes made the cupbearer an influential and sought-after messenger. A shrewd cupbearer could parlay his influence into a fortune. That's why the position called for a man of integrity, a man who would not easily sell out. Nehemiah was such a man.

The job was not without hazards, either. Each time Nehemiah served the king his cup, he would carefully ladle out a sample and drink it to prove that he believed it was not poisoned. Of course, if someone else *had* poisoned it, he would suffer the consequences.

Obviously the job of cupbearer, though it was a servant's task, was not menial. Nehemiah had a daily audience with the king, something not even the king's closest advisors could count on. He lived in the royal palace and ate the same food as the king.

But Nehemiah's heart was with his people, the Jews. He had not become haughty because of the benefits of his job; he had not begun to identify so much with the privileges of royalty that he forgot where he came from. God had brought him to the kingdom for just such a time as this.

The Awakening of a Champion

Nehemiah 1:2–3 tells what happened to start Nehemiah on his marvelous quest:

> Hanani one of my brethren came with men from Judah; and I asked them concerning the Jews who had escaped, who had survived the captivity, and concerning Jerusalem. And they said to me, "The survivors who are left from the captivity in the province are there in great distress and reproach. The

wall of Jerusalem is also broken down, and its gates
are burned with fire."

That message set his heart on fire! The people of Jerusalem were in great affliction and reproach. Why? Because the wall of the city was a pile of rubble, and the gates
were splinters and ashes. In the ancient world, a city without secure walls and gates was a nonentity.

Jerusalem was a laughingstock. And worse than that,
the name of the Lord was being mocked because His people were being ridiculed. They were the brunt of God's
enemies' jokes. Not only was the unwalled city vulnerable
to enemies' attacks and marauders' raids, but the nation's
testimony for the Lord lay in ruins alongside those crumbled walls.

It would have been easy for Nehemiah to sit back, dis-
miss the whole thing, and say, "Oh, well. That's their
problem. I've got enough to worry about here in the comfort of my palace. I might be drinking poison." He might
have told them, "Now, listen, boys, I've got to put on my
royal garments, because the emperor is waiting for me.
Nobody keeps the emperor waiting, you know. Glad to see
you. Tell the servants I said to give you some food, and
God bless you. I will be praying for you."

But that wouldn't have been the response of a champion.

Remember Psalm 137, the song about the Jews' con-
tempt for their captors? Perhaps Nehemiah was familiar
with verses 5–6 of that psalm: "If I forget you, O Jerusalem, let my right hand forget her skill! If I do not remem-

ber you, let my tongue cling to the roof of my mouth—if I do not exalt Jerusalem above my chief joy."

Nehemiah, as a man of character, could not turn his back on his people or their city. The news he received that day awakened the champion in him and started him on an adventure that would set the course of his nation's history until the time of Christ. As he listened to the sorrows and needs of the great city of God, the mystery of greatness descended to stir his soul. He no longer desired the royal courts of Persia. He no longer desired the beautiful garments he wore. He no longer wanted to greet ambassadors from other nations and bring their gifts to the king. All of that became nothing to him. He was ready to lay it all on the line to serve the Lord and His people.

Do you think he realized at that point that he would be a champion? I don't. I don't believe he felt he was special in any way—certainly he didn't view himself as the most qualified person to lead an army of bricklayers! As he looked at the task before him, his vision was filled with the omnipotence of God. When he thought of Jerusalem, he wasn't seeing a gigantic wall. He was seeing the God who is greater than all the stones and mortar ever made.

David was just like that in the face of mighty Goliath. Where everyone else saw an unconquerable giant, he saw only an "uncircumcised Philistine" who had the audacity to "defy the armies of the living God" (1 Sam. 17:26). David didn't see himself as better equipped than anyone else to kill Goliath. He just couldn't understand why everyone else stood idly by and watched as this mere giant challenged the great God of Israel. It wasn't that David thought of himself as a champion. But he knew the power of God.

Everyone else looked at Goliath and thought, *He's too big to defeat*. But David saw him and thought, *He's so big, I can't possibly miss!* By faith he strode into the presence of the giant armed only with a slingshot and some pebbles. And he made a deep impression on Goliath, to say the least.

One Plus God Is a Majority

It's amazing what God can do with one person, any person, who will abdicate prestige, position, status, and his or her own will—and consecrate his or her life solely to being all the Lord wants. God working through an ordinary person can overcome seemingly insurmountable obstacles and accomplish incredible feats. It is true that one plus God is always a majority.

I think of the story of another layman, a young shoe salesman in New England who came to Christ in the 1800s. He applied for membership to a Boston church but was rejected because he couldn't explain the basics of the gospel. The young man determined to study so that he could be used of God to teach others. His business took him to Chicago, where he joined a church and asked to be permitted to teach a Sunday school class. The Sunday school superintendent was put off by his crude and uneducated manner, so he told him there were no openings. He suggested that the young man try to recruit his own students. That's exactly what he did, and soon his Sunday school was the world's largest.

This young man began to devote more and more of his time to reaching people with the gospel. When the demands of his evangelistic work became so great that he could no longer keep his job, he left the business world and went to work for the Lord full time. He lost everything in the great Chicago fire, so he went to England to try to raise money to rebuild. It was there that he heard a man say, "The world has yet to see what God can do through a man wholly consecrated to Him." The immediate response of the young man's heart was, "By the grace of God, I'll be that man."

That man was D. L. Moody, and God used him to reach two powerful nations for Christ. Although he was an unschooled layman, he founded schools and churches to raise up others for full-time service. But he remained a layman until the end of his life. Even after he had preached to thousands all over England and America, he still insisted on being called *Mr*. Moody, not Reverend or Pastor. He was just a layman with a passion to serve the Lord. His influence continues today, almost a century after his ministry ended.

God delights to use ordinary people. And when God puts his hand on a man or woman, watch out! There's no limit to what He can accomplish.

You see, God's strength is made perfect through our weaknesses (see 2 Cor. 12:9). He accomplishes His greatest victories through us at precisely the points where we are the weakest. That's because we're more likely to let go and let God work when we're most painfully aware of the likelihood of our own failure.

Nehemiah knew that. He had never been a builder, but God used him to build. He had never been a ruler, but God used him to govern Israel. He had never been a clergyman, but God used him to take a nation by the heart and lift its people up to spiritual heights they had not known for centuries.

God's ways are not our ways. We look for a Saul, a man of stature, to be our leader. God sends us a young shepherd boy like David. We seek a mighty, conquering messiah. God gives us an infant in a manger. His strength is always made perfect in weakness.

Don't be fooled into thinking that you don't have what it takes to be a champion. That's not even an issue. The wonderful truth is, God can do whatever He must do to *make* you a champion. Who you are and what you have are unimportant; what you let God do *through* you is what counts. Let God make you a true champion.

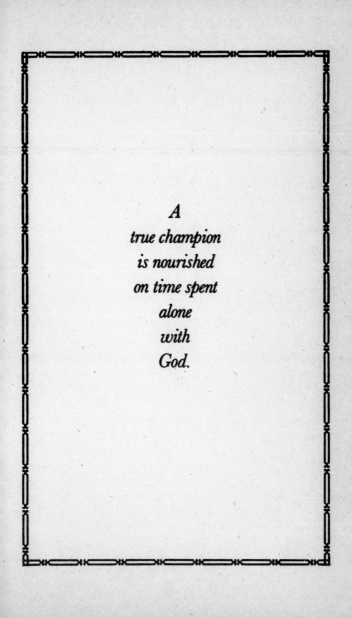

*A
true champion
is nourished
on time spent
alone
with
God.*

3

Breakfast of Champions

Nehemiah had made up his mind to do something about those ruined walls. He must have wanted to rush wildly into the court of the king and plead for help. But instead he walked boldly into the presence of God and begged for mercy.

The first chapter of Nehemiah is almost completely given to a record of Nehemiah's prayer. Turning to the last chapter of the book, we find also that the final verses close with prayer. Everything in between is thus bracketed with wonderful insight into how a choice servant of God poured out his heart before the Almighty. And that's fitting, because prayer was an important key to Nehemiah's success. At least eleven times in the book of Nehemiah, we see him kneeling before God in prayer.

A true champion is nourished on time spent alone with

God. He gets his sustenance for the day, not at the break-fast table, but in the prayer closet. Prayer is more important to him than food when it comes to energy for serving God, and before he can go forth to do some great work for the Lord, he must first retreat to Him in prayer.

God won't use a man who loves to put himself on a pedestal before men; He chooses instead those who spend time on their knees before the throne of grace.

The litmus test of any person's spiritual character is his prayer life. Real success comes not from the work we do when the world is watching, but from the life we live when no one can see. No man or woman who fails at prayer can be truly successful at any endeavor for God. Regardless of what your gift is, no matter what God has called you to do, the secret to ultimate victory is the victory you gain in secret. The most important aspect of your calling is your prayer life.

We are all called to pray. Not everyone can preach or be a missionary, but everyone does have the privilege of prayer. Yet it's interesting, isn't it, that most of us consider ourselves failures at private prayer? If you want to humble the average Christian leader, all you have to do is ask him about his prayer life.

But there was nothing average about Nehemiah as far as his prayer life was concerned. Prayer was as natural to him as breathing. So when faced with the greatest challenge of his life, he turned immediately to the Lord.

Building a Wall on a Foundation of Prayer

Nehemiah's prayer was in no sense a cop-out. It wasn't that he was afraid to act—he was a man of action. When the Lord laid it on his heart to rebuild the walls of Jerusalem, he must have found it very difficult not to quit his job immediately and get going. But he knew better. Notice that between Nehemiah 1:1 and 2:1, four months passed. During that time he treasured his secret ambition in his heart and didn't even tell the king. This man of action was first of all a man of prayer.

There's a great lesson here. When we're inclined to act, we are usually better off to bathe our desires in prayer first. Nehemiah didn't see prayer as inactivity or use it to avoid real involvement; he saw it as the only basis for holy activity and righteous involvement. If he was going to build a wall for God, he was going to build it on a solid foundation of prayer.

This is a principle I've tried to abide by over the years. I realized long ago that things done in haste usually go wrong. No decision is so urgent that there's no time to pray it through. The greater the impact of the decision, the more time I spend before the Lord, asking Him to direct my thoughts and help me make a wise decision. I never want to be forced into a hasty decision without adequate time in prayer, no matter how pressing circumstances may seem. On the other hand, once I've made a decision, I move rapidly and determinedly to do what I'm convinced God wants me to do.

Four months is a long time for a man of action to wait. But in the scope of all that Nehemiah accomplished, those four months before God, time spent planning and praying about what he should do, represented perhaps the most fruitful time of all. That was where he cultivated the character and conviction he would need when opposition threatened to level the walls even while he was still building them.

The Prayer of a Godly Man

Nehemiah 1:4 shows how this man of God responded to the devastating news that the crumbled city walls had become a reproach: "So it was, when I heard these words, that I sat down and wept, and mourned for many days; I was fasting and praying before the God of heaven."

Notice the five key verbs in that brief passage: *sat down, wept, mourned, fasting,* and *praying.* There's a sweet progression there, as Nehemiah absorbed the tremendous shock of learning an awful truth. As we will see in chapter 5 of this book, Nehemiah, for all his determination to get going and rebuild the walls, was a man of true compassion and deep feeling. He had to weep and mourn over the ruins before he could rebuild the fallen walls.

Dealing with his grief in a righteous manner, he turned to the One who he knew permitted the calamity. He humbly asked Him for mercy to forgive the sins of a nation and restore their former glory.

The nation's sin was the real issue, not the ruined walls. Nehemiah was quick to grasp that truth. Interestingly, in the entire prayer, Nehemiah never once mentioned the walls of Jerusalem. The real shame of Jerusalem was not that her walls were piles of crumbled stone overgrown with weeds. It was that her people had turned from their

God and were living under His judgment. Therein lay the greater reproach, and Nehemiah knew it.

So Nehemiah's prayer was a prayer of repentance. The key words are "we have sinned" (v. 6). He rehearsed the promises of God and the failures of his people, always acknowledging the righteousness of God in His judgment on a sinning nation. But he pleaded also for mercy.

Talking to God in His Own Language

The language of Nehemiah's prayer shows that he was intimately familiar with the Word of God. He spoke in biblical terms, and he recited biblical history. That's the best kind of prayer, because it is talking to God in His own language.

Nehemiah began with confession. "If we confess our sins, He is faithful and just to forgive us our sins and to cleanse us from all unrighteousness" (1 John 1:9). *Confess* in that verse means "say the same thing as." Real confession means agreeing with God about our sin—again, speaking to Him in His own language.

There was no self-righteous posturing in Nehemiah's words, either. Wherever he mentioned the nation's guilt, he used the first-person pronouns: "me," "I," "my," "ours." The guilt he felt was personal as well as national. Perhaps that explains the depth of his grief and the length of time he spent in mourning and fasting.

Here was a man qualified to lead God's people. Instead of standing apart from them and pointing to their sin, he stood with them and bore the weight of their guilt. Isn't that what Jesus did for us?

Nehemiah's willingness to identify with the failings of

his people is one of the keys to his effectiveness. Later in his ministry, when Nehemiah would face opposition, his people would stand with him. Why were they willing to do that? Because Nehemiah set the example by making himself one of them.

All truly great leaders stand with their people, even in difficulty. None of us has any respect for the boss who tries to cover himself by blaming his subordinates for problems. A good leader doesn't do that. He accepts responsibility for his people's failures as one of the prices of leadership. Instead of standing over his subordinates trying to intimidate them into submission, he comes alongside them and helps to bear the burden, even if that means sharing the blame for their failure.

Taking God at His Word

Having confessed his sin and the sin of the people, Nehemiah claimed the promises of God. One of the greatest advantages of knowing the Scripture and praying to God in biblical terms is that you can recite His promises and claim them.

"Remember, I pray, the word that You commanded Your servant Moses" (v. 8). Why did Nehemiah say that? Did God need to be reminded of His promise? No. Would He have failed to keep His word if Nehemiah had not reminded Him of it? No.

Prayer is not for God's benefit, but for ours. We are commanded to pray, not because God needs the information or the attention, but because we need the experience of knowing and demonstrating that we depend on Him.

God is glorified when He can respond specifically to our prayers. It bolsters our faith and strengthens us when He grants what we ask for. And it reinforces in us the knowledge that we depend solely on Him.

As Nehemiah poured out his heart to God, we see that he was taking God totally at His word. What a marvelous man of faith he was! Consider this: those walls had lain in ruins for decades. Other men had come and gone, and they had had access to the same promises of Scripture that Nehemiah was now reciting back to God. Why had no one else had the faith to seek God's direction in the rebuilding of the fallen walls? Because they were not men of vision.

A man of prayer is always a man of vision. The more he prays, the more intimately he knows God. The more intimately he knows God, the more able he is to see things with a divine perspective. And a man who sees things with a divine perspective is a man of great vision.

Calling the Things that Are Not as though They Were

Because Nehemiah was man of vision, he was able to look at the piles of crumbled stones and see walls. He looked at the heaps of ashes and saw new gates. He saw things that other men could not.

God always uses people who can see beyond what seems to be and grasp the vision of a greater reality. That is the essence of faith.

George Mueller, who ran an orphanage in nineteenth-century Bristol, England, was a man of vision. He made it a policy never to reveal his financial needs to anyone. Even when people asked, he would tell only the Lord what the needs were. He saw God as his ultimate provider, and he believed that if God was in the ministry, He would lay it on people's hearts to participate. One man, visiting the orphanage, said to Mueller, "Of course you cannot carry on these institutions without a good stock of funds."

Mueller acknowledged that that was the case.

"Have you a good stock?" the man asked.

Mueller, knowing that he was penniless, only answered quietly, "Our funds are deposited in a bank which cannot break."

The man responded by saying he wanted to make an investment in that bank, and he gave Mueller a sizable gift.

Many times when Mueller had no money, no food, and no knowledge of where the orphans' next meal would come from, he would nevertheless gather them around the table at mealtime and thank the Lord for His gracious provision. On more than one occasion, while they were yet praying, an unexpected donor would show up with food enough for everyone.

I've seen this happen in my ministry, too. As a young preacher, sensing the call of God to preach the gospel to the world, I left San Francisco on a ship with only twelve dollars in my pocket. That was all I had, except for enough faith to believe that the God who had called me could also provide my needs along the way. He did, and I learned that God's provision is one thing that is a certainty. The eyes of faith lay hold of what God has promised to do, not what the natural eyes see happening.

The apostle Paul, writing about the faith of Abraham, said he trusted a God who "calls those things which do not exist as though they did" (Rom. 4:17). What would we normally say about someone who calls things that are not as though they were? We would say he is a liar. But not so with God. He can call the things that are not as though they are because He knows the end from the beginning (see Isa. 46:10). That means He knows how things will turn out from the time they start. He looks into the future and sees the culmination of all He's going to do. The future is so certain with Him that He counts it as an accomplished fact and declares it to be so.

That's how God could look at a trembling Gideon and see a mighty man of valor. He can look at sinners like you and me and call us righteous. He looked at Jerusalem's tumbled-down boulders and heaps of broken stones—and He pronounced them a wall.

Nehemiah shared that vision. He didn't run from the awesome task of rebuilding the wall, because with the eyes of faith he saw it as already completed. He knew God would keep His word, because he was on intimate terms with God.

A Hint of Things to Come

As we have noted, Nehemiah didn't specifically mention the walls of Jerusalem in his prayer. But in his petition, we can catch a glimmer of the fire that had ignited his heart. In the final verse of his prayer (v. 11), he mentioned two requests: first, "let Your servant prosper this day, I pray," and second, "grant him mercy in the sight of this man."

The prayer for prosperity hinted that Nehemiah was planning to do something that had a risk of failure. God knew what he meant, and we do, too. He was going to rebuild those walls. But for that he needed his present employer's permission. That explains the second request. "This man" whose mercy he sought was King Artaxerxes. Nehemiah was going to enter his presence and ask for a great favor. If the king got angry, Nehemiah could lose his job, be imprisoned, or even forfeit his life.

Were the walls of a city he had never even seen worth such a risk? You bet. Nehemiah had discovered his life's calling, and nothing was going to deter him. No matter how high the stakes, he was prepared to ante up. He wanted to be everything God could make him.

A Leap of Faith—with the Eyes Wide Open

This was not a rash decision. Remember, Nehemiah had fasted and prayed and mourned "for many days" (v. 4). Though he was decisive, Nehemiah was not impetuous. He had prayed through his decision, and he never wavered from it. So when the time came to approach the king, he did it from a solid basis of faith.

He wasn't reacting from emotion, although it's clear that he felt deeply about what he was doing. He wasn't operating in a reactionary mode; he had carefully considered his course, and now that it was time to take the leap of faith, he was doing it with his eyes open.

That is one of the ultimate benefits of prayer, I'm convinced. It trains us to go over our options, to pray through every angle of a decision, and to see things more clearly through the eyes of faith. Have you ever made a bad decision because you didn't take the time to pray it through? I have. I remember clearly when a church in South Bend, Indiana, approached me about being their pastor. I flatly told them no, I wasn't interested. I felt God had called me to a different area of ministry. Besides, I wasn't particularly attracted to South Bend.

The next night, I received another call from the South Bend church. The man on the other end told me that the church people had fasted and prayed all day and once again had voted unanimously to call me.

"That's very interesting," I said. "I appreciate that very much, but I can't come." And I hung up.

The next night another call came from the church. They were convinced I hadn't prayed about my decision. If I prayed it through, they felt, I would change my mind. They were right, and I accepted the call.

Several years later, after I had left South Bend to spend several years overseas, the Lord gave me an almost identical decision to consider. I had recently returned to the United States and was seeking the Lord's will about a location for our international headquarters. One day I received a telephone call asking me to come back to South Bend to begin a new church there. Sixty-nine people, who were meeting in a basement and had no pastor, had signed a petition asking me to come be their spiritual leader. I told them I could not make a quick decision. My former church, located in a different part of South Bend, was still going strong. I couldn't see going back to start from scratch again.

But this time, I knew better than to try to make the

decision without spending time in prayer. After seeking the Lord's will diligently on my knees, I knew what He wanted me to do. I said yes to the group in South Bend, and our ministry has been located there ever since.

More often than I can remember, I have been saved from a bad decision because I took the time to pray it through. In the course of praying, I saw things more clearly from God's perspective. Just as often I have experienced what Nehemiah did. After a season of prayer about something I feel deeply for, I find myself more committed than ever to what I began to pray for. Either way, prayer enables us to see things in sharper focus through the eyes of faith.

A Lesson from Our Lord

Do we really need to cultivate a life of prayer? Consider this: our Lord, while He was here on earth, rose up in the morning, "a long while before daylight," to go to a place where He could be alone and pray (Mark 1:35).

The Lord Jesus had none of the shortcomings with which we suffer. He knew the Father as intimately as it is possible to know Him. He said, "I and My Father are one" (John 10:30). He knew God's will perfectly, and He did not struggle with weak faith as we do.

Yet prayer was important to Him. He prayed early in the morning. He would go into the wilderness to pray. He prayed before the transfiguration. He prayed in the garden the night he was betrayed. Prayer was a hallmark of His daily life. Why? Because even as the omnipotent, omniscient God in human flesh, He drew His power from the Father. "The Son can do nothing of Himself, but what He sees the Father do" (John 5:19).

He voluntarily laid aside His right to do anything independently, and He completely subjugated Himself to the will of the Father. He depended on the Father. He obeyed the Father. He looked to the Father for everything. And the means by which Jesus kept in touch with the Father was prayer.

If Jesus needed to pray, how much more do we? He never had a sin to confess. He had no confusion to untangle. And He never needed to pray for healing or deliverance. Yet He prayed constantly—and left us an example to follow.

No Walls without a Foundation

I'm convinced that if Nehemiah had not spent a season in prayer, he never would have built those walls. How can you build a wall without a proper foundation?

If Nehemiah had not tarried before the Lord prior to going out to put up the walls, he surely would have lacked the strength to withstand the trials he encountered later. Had he not been energized by prayer, he would have burned out long before the walls were finished.

How's *your* prayer life? You've been afraid I was going to ask that, haven't you? If you're like everyone else I know, you'll admit that you lose a lot of battles when it comes to prayer.

But prayer is the place where our greatest battles *must* be won. If we lose the battle before we pray, we've lost the battle completely. The victory Nehemiah won in prayer here became the basis for all his victories on the wall. That's how it is with us. The foundation of prayer we lay becomes a platform on which all our other victories can ultimately stand.

And that's the marvelous thing about prayer. It's so far-reaching. The effects of prayer do not know the bounds of distance or time. We can pray for something near or far in the future. We can pray for our next-door neighbor, or for someone halfway around the world. The effect is the same. God hears the prayer of faith and glorifies Himself in the answer.

Early in my ministry, I once became very ill while traveling between China and Tibet. I was riding on a donkey in a caravan when I became so weak I could not go on. I had been bleeding and feverish for nearly two days, and I was severely dehydrated. I dismounted, tied my donkey to a tree, and lay down to die. Almost immediately I passed out.

I don't know how long I was unconscious, but when I finally awoke, I was fine. The fever was gone, and my strength was back. It took me a full day to catch up with the caravan, but I finally did locate them that evening at dusk. Just before I went to sleep that night, I recorded in my diary, "I lay down to die, and God healed me."

More than two years later, while I was in Mobile, Alabama, to visit my mother, I was sharing some of my diary entries with her Christian women's group. A dear woman in that group showed me her own diary. Written there was an account of how at 10:00 P.M. on the day before I almost died in Tibet, she had been strongly impressed to pray for me. She had prayed fervently that the Lord would not let me die. Her diary showed that she had prayed for nearly two hours before she felt certain I was all right. Then she made the diary entry before she went to bed for the evening.

At 10:00 P.M. in Mobile, Alabama, it is 10:00 A.M. the following day in Tibet. In other words, at the exact time that woman was praying, I was lying under a tree unconscious, halfway around the world! God had guided her in her praying, and He had glorified Himself by answering.

Prayer does indeed change things. It changes us. It strengthens our faith. It helps us to see things through God's eyes. It softens our hearts. It sensitizes our consciences. It gives us superhuman courage. And it molds us into champions God can use.

How *is* your prayer life?

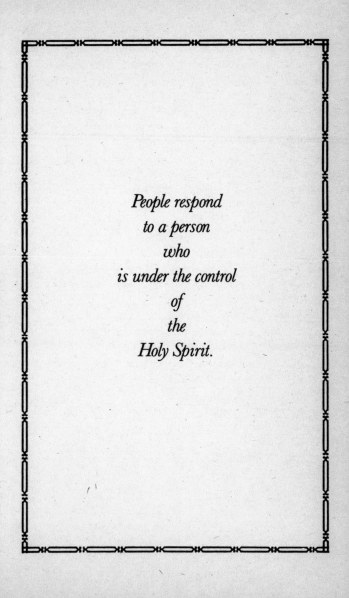

*People respond
to a person
who
is under the control
of
the
Holy Spirit.*

4

Power from a Higher Source

*T*ransforming miles of boulders and weed-covered rubble into city walls must have seemed an impossible task. Maybe that's why no one before Nehemiah had tackled the job. But from start to finish, Nehemiah's work took less than two months.

Two months is so brief and the wall is so large that skeptics have pointed to Nehemiah's account for centuries as evidence that the biblical record is not credible. But the skeptics of our day are nothing new; Nehemiah had plenty of detractors telling him the job was impossible, even while he was in the midst of doing it.

How could a mere man organize a team of formerly uncommitted people and coordinate the effort to pull off such a herculean task in so short a time? The answer, of course, is that a mere man could not have done it on his own. Nehemiah was a man empowered by God.

What set Nehemiah apart from the average person was that he was called by God, controlled by the Holy Spirit, energized by divine power, and totally yielded to God's will. Nothing can stop such a person from accomplishing whatever God sets before him or her to do.

Called by God

Does it strike you as unusual that Nehemiah spent four months praying about a job he would ultimately complete in less than two? If there was such a hurry to get the walls up, why did he tarry in prayer for so long? Surely one reason was that before he undertook such an enormous commitment, he wanted to be certain of the call of God on his life.

He was wise to invest that time confirming God's call. It's easy in a moment of reactive zeal to get excited about serving God and set out on some quest that is in itself worthwhile but has nothing to do with what God is calling us to do. I'm sure that's the reason a lot of missionaries burn out or return from the mission field early. Perhaps they were never called to go in the first place.

Jesus taught that before we do anything, we should count the cost: "For which of you, intending to build a tower, does not sit down first and count the cost, whether he has enough to finish it—lest, after he has laid the foundation, and is not able to finish it, all who see it begin to mock him, saying, 'This man began to build and was not able to finish'" (Luke 14:28–30).

Our Lord applied that truth to would-be disciples. Those who came to Him without first counting the cost were sent away: "And another also said, 'Lord, I will follow You, but let me first go and bid them farewell who are at my house.' But Jesus said to him, 'No one, having put his hand to the plow, and looking back, is fit for the kingdom of God'" (Luke 9:61–62).

Counting the cost has a way of eliminating those who are not really called.

God will frequently call a person to a task for which he or she is not humanly qualified. That was the case with Nehemiah. He wasn't qualified to build a wall. He was a servant, not a leader. He was a man with a comfortable job, not a laborer. He was accustomed to life in the palace, not long, hot days in the desert sun. He lived in Shushan, not Jerusalem. Why would God call him to go and build a wall around a city he had never seen?

The cost to Nehemiah was high. But after four months in prayer—time he must have spent planning and counting the cost—he knew God had called him to rebuild that wall, and no price was too high.

No price is ever too high when God calls a person. We may be asked to give up riches, family, or other temporal things, but God will always bless us with more than we give up.

Billy Sunday was one of the world's best-known baseball players when he was converted. He could run the bases faster than any man who had ever played the game. Everyone in America knew his name. He had fame, money, status, and everything he had ever longed for. Then the Lord called him into ministry.

Sunday never thought twice about whether he should leave baseball to go into the ministry. He gave it all up to serve the Lord. For the first ten years of his ministry, Sunday ministered in the shadows. He was an assistant to another evangelist, and he preached in rescue missions and small churches. Many people thought he had squandered great potential in professional sports to become a third-rate preacher.

But God had called Billy Sunday to serve Him. Like Moses, Sunday spent some years in training on the backside of the desert. When a person responds so readily to God's call, God uses him to the utmost. After a few years of ministry in obscurity, Sunday was on the front lines. He became the best-known evangelist in America, and he was instrumental in the conversions of tens of thousands of souls.

Nehemiah had a similar sense of destiny. It seems he never questioned God's call, and he never hesitated about obeying it.

How can we know Nehemiah was certain of God's call? First of all, God must have confirmed it in his heart during those months spent in prayer. Second, it was a pretty good indicator when Nehemiah appeared before the king and asked for permission to go to Jerusalem, and the king agreed! Nehemiah took a great risk in asking. The king could have viewed the request as presumptuous or even treasonous. Just by asking, Nehemiah was risking his job, his freedom—even his life. So when the king granted permission and furthermore offered help, that confirmed God's call to Nehemiah.

But more than that, Nehemiah sensed the call in his inner man. His heart was so burdened with the task of building the wall that he could scarcely think of anything else. He knew God's hand was upon him. He was anointed to build the wall, and he no longer had the desire to do anything else. Writing about his appeal to the king, Nehemiah recorded, "And the king granted them to me *according to the good hand of my God upon me*" (2:8, emphasis added). By the time he stepped into the presence of the king, there was no doubt in Nehemiah's mind about whether God had called him. God's hand was upon him, and he could sense it.

That's how it is when God calls a person. When I sensed the call of God to worldwide evangelism, all my other desires left me. All I wanted to do was preach. I have to admit that in the early days I didn't always enjoy preaching, but I could never have given a moment's thought to anything else. Despite all the hardships and obstacles of those early years, I knew God had called me. With that knowledge, I could face almost any challenge, including the ridicule and disparagement of friends and relatives.

In fact, shortly after I answered God's call to the ministry, I set out on a tour of the world by faith, trusting the Lord to provide food, shelter, and places to preach. He provided wonderfully, and although I had never gone to college, I got a wonderful education in the school of faith—the same school Nehemiah attended to learn how to build a wall.

After he arrived at Jerusalem, Nehemiah spent three days studying the walls, planning what he would do, without telling anyone why he was there. Noting that, he wrote, "I told no one what my *God had put in my heart to do* at Jerusalem" (2:12, emphasis added). It's clear that he saw his burden to rebuild the walls as a desire put in his heart by God Himself. That's what it's like to be called by God.

I spent many years serving the Lord in the Philippines. I was certain of God's call to minister there, and I was just as certain of God's direction when he called me to return to America to minister on television. But the first preacher I met when I got to the United States said to me, "Sumrall, you're fifty and you're finished."

His words hurt, but I knew in my heart what God had called me to do. I went into a prayer room and I said, "Lord, did You hear that preacher? He says I'm fifty and finished. Does he know what he's talking about?"

God confirmed His call in my heart once again that day. "You're not finished," God said. "You're just getting started. Run with your vision." And from that day I have never had a doubt about God's call on my life.

I could have listened to that man. I might have run out and bought a rocking chair and sat in the corner and rocked until I died. But I would have missed the most marvelous years of service the Lord has ever given me. The call of God may differ from the opinions of men, but if we are going to serve God, His call is what counts.

Controlled by the Holy Spirit

God's call is important, but that's not all there is to being used mightily by God. God calls many people who never respond, or who answer the call but never yield control of their lives to the Holy Spirit. If Nehemiah had tried to build those massive walls according to his own plan and in his own energy, the piles of rubble and stones might be there to this day. He didn't have the wherewithal to do it by himself. But as a man controlled by the Spirit of God, Nehemiah was destined to do things greater than his human potential indicated.

Although Nehemiah spent much time in prayer and preparation for his task, he never wavered from his calling. Don't interpret his times in prayer and solitude as hesitation. Nothing in the Bible indicates that Nehemiah ever faced a moment's indecision. On the contrary, the picture we get of him is one of a man who is decisive, determined, devoid of any doubt about where he's going and what he's going to do.

There's a good reason for that: Nehemiah was clearly under the control of the Holy Spirit.

A significant exchange took place toward the end of Nehemiah 2, when Nehemiah first confronted his countrymen with the full details of what he was there to do. "I told them of the hand of my God which had been good upon me," he wrote in verse 18. "So they said, 'Let us rise up and build.'"

Don't read through that verse so quickly that you miss its significance. Remember, the Jews living in Jerusalem had been coming back from captivity for nearly a hundred years. Rebuilding the Temple had been a major undertaking, a job that took more than twenty years. No one in all those years had had the heart to take on the chore of reconstructing the crumbled walls, even though the piles of broken stones were the first sight that greeted every visitor. The debris around the city made Jerusalem and the whole Jewish nation the object of ridicule. No one liked being the brunt of a bad joke, but building those walls seemed such an impossible task.

After all those years, how could Nehemiah walk into town, challenge the people to rebuild the walls, and get an immediate positive response, "Let us rise up and build"? The answer is right there in verse 18: "I told them of the hand of my God which had been good upon me." They could see that God was using him. It was obvious to everyone that this man was anointed by God for this task. And people respond to a person who is under the control of the Holy Spirit.

All the human energy and motivation in the world could not have moved those people to tackle the rebuilding of the walls. They had lived in the shadow of those broken walls for years. They were accustomed to the jokes. They weren't going to respond lightly to this fellow from out of town, no matter how impassioned he was or how urgently he felt the city needed walls.

But when they heard Nehemiah speak, they were listening to another voice—the still, small voice of the Holy Spirit, who controlled Nehemiah. He had never read Ephesians 5:18, but Nehemiah was a Spirit-filled man.

It's impossible to stress too much the importance of being filled with the Holy Spirit. When Ephesians 5:18 says, "Be filled with the Spirit," it's giving us a command, not an option. It carries the same weight as the preceding phrase, "Do not be drunk with wine." Most Christians wouldn't think of getting drunk, but did you realize that "Be filled with the Spirit" is a part of the same command? You may not be a drunkard, but if you are not filled with the Holy Spirit, you are living in disobedience just the same.

Why do you suppose that verse links drunkenness with being Spirit-filled? It's a stark contrast, for one thing, but there are some parallels, too. To be filled with the Spirit is to be under His influence, controlled by the Spirit of God so much that He directs our actions, words, and thoughts.

When Scripture says we need to be filled with the Spirit, it doesn't mean that we need *more* of the Spirit, but rather that we need to *yield* more of ourselves to Him. The expression "filled with the Spirit" is like the phrases "filled with wrath" (Luke 4:28); "fill[ed] . . . with all joy and peace" (Rom. 15:13); or even "drunk with wine." It means to be completely controlled by something else, so that you give up control of yourself.

Nehemiah was controlled by the Spirit of God in that sense. He had so yielded his heart, soul, mind, and strength to God that he was completely under the influence of the Holy Spirit. Until then, the hardest work his hands had done had been to carry a tray of food to the king. But now those hands were about to be used by the One who created the stars and planets from nothing. And a pile of rocks and broken mortar are nothing to hands under the control of the God of the universe.

Energized by Divine Power

Nehemiah had an unlimited power source from which to draw. He knew it, and he must have known that God, having called him to do this great work, would also supply him with the supernatural strength to carry it out.

Isn't that the essence of great faith? It is the ability to lay hold of God's strength to do something that would otherwise be impossible. Jesus said, "If you have faith as a mustard seed, you will say to this mountain, 'Move from here to there,' and it will move; and nothing will be impossible for you" (Matt. 17:20).

Nehemiah was facing an impossible mountain of rubble. Yet he never seemed to doubt that he could move that mountain from where it was to where it should be. After all, he was called by God, controlled by the Holy Spirit, and confident that God would supply whatever strength he needed to obey.

Here's a key principle to remember: God does not ask us to do anything that He will not also empower us to do. Don't say, "But I can't witness for Christ. I'm too shy." God has commanded you to witness, and He will enable you to do it. Don't say, "But I can't love my husband." God has commanded you to love him, and He will give you the power to do it.

God's will may not always be easy, but it is never impossible. It may *look* impossible, but the God of the Bible specializes in making impossibilities happen. Jesus would look at a paraplegic and say, "Arise, take up your bed, and go to your house" (Matt. 9:6); or encounter a man with a shriveled arm and say, "Stretch out your hand" (Matt. 12:13). He asked them to do the very things they were powerless to do! But with the command to do it always comes the power to obey. That's how God always works.

Nehemiah spent his first three days in Jerusalem secretly surveying the walls. He saw rugged rocks. He saw tattered bits. He saw complete disarray all around where the wall had once stood. Nehemiah 2:13–16 describes his night missions:

And I went out by night through the Valley Gate to the Serpent Well and the Refuse Gate, and viewed the walls of Jerusalem which were broken down and its gates which were burned with fire. Then I went on to the Fountain Gate and to the King's Pool, but there was no room for the animal that was under me to pass. So I went up in the night by the valley, and viewed the wall; then I turned back and entered by the Valley Gate, and so returned. And the officials did not know where I had gone or what I had done; I had not yet told the Jews.

That would have been enough to discourage the average person. You and I would have probably shrugged our shoulders and left Jerusalem on the first camel back to Shushan. Not Nehemiah. He came back from studying the walls more excited than ever about what God had called him to do. He told the Israelites he recruited to help him, "The God of heaven Himself will prosper us" (2:20). He had seen the walls for the first time, and he had looked at them through the eyes of faith. He saw marvelous walls with secure gates, not heaps of rocks and burned wood. *God* was going to build those walls, and He had chosen Nehemiah to oversee the work.

Totally Yielded to God's Will

Nehemiah drew his strength from an endless resource. What other men saw as obstacles, he laid hold of as wonderful opportunities. He had seen the plight of Jerusalem firsthand. It was no longer just a rumor he had heard. He now knew for himself what an exacting task he had accepted. But the total effect of all that on him was only to make him more determined to do God's will.

Nehemiah 2 introduces us to two names we will see again in Nehemiah's saga: Sanballat and Tobiah. Nehemiah recorded in verse 10 that "they were deeply disturbed that a man had come to seek the well-being of the children of Israel." They couldn't stand it that Nehemiah was on the side of God's people. These were contemptible, worthless men, determined to thwart Nehemiah's work through whatever means they could.

Their first act was to hold Nehemiah and his fellow workers up to public ridicule. Nehemiah 2:19 says, "They laughed us to scorn and despised us, and said, 'What is this thing that you are doing? Will you rebel against the king?'"

Nehemiah wasn't rebelling against the king. He had the king's permission and encouragement to build the walls. But he didn't even say so. That wasn't the most important thing to Nehemiah. He was doing the will of God.

Nehemiah was consumed with a passion to glorify God by doing His will. From the day he heard that the walls were broken down, Nehemiah ceased to care about his own comfort, his own desires, his own future. All he wanted to do was get those walls up—not because he would gain anything from it, but because God would be glorified.

Nehemiah didn't mind the calluses, he didn't care that he would get dirty, he didn't pay any attention to the ridicule and scorn that was heaped on him. He was doing God's will, and that was all that mattered.

How about you? Are there some piles of rubble in your life that God wants you to turn into monuments to His glory? Are you overwhelmed by the size of the task He has set before you? Are you feeling He has called you to do something impossible?

Your frustration can be turned to great victory with a simple change of perspective. Look at yourself as a tool in the hand of God—a power tool. A carpenter can't operate his electrical tools properly unless they are plugged into the power source. Oh, if he worked long enough, he might be able to cut a board in half with a juiceless power saw, but it would take him at least a hundred times as long, and the cut wouldn't be as clean.

That's how it is with us. Without God's power, we bungle everything we try to do for Him. But if we reach out by faith and claim that power, we can be effective instruments in His hand to change the world. And that's what He made us for.

Like Nehemiah, you are a person of destiny. God is calling you to serve Him, and with His call comes the power to obey. You'll be amazed to find what God will do in and through you if you plug into His power.

*Real compassion
is a critical part
of truly great
character.*

5

You Gotta Have Heart

*F*ormer President Harry Truman defined leadership as the ability to get men to do what they don't want to do and like it. I like that definition. It's a rare person, indeed, who can motivate people to do what they don't want to do and in the process make them enjoy the thing they had previously avoided.

That's exactly what Nehemiah did, however. The inhabitants of Jerusalem were apathetic about their ruined walls. No one wanted to undertake the job of rebuilding those walls. People were busy enough without that. They had to plow their fields, sell their wares, provide for their families. A civic building project would just be an expensive, time-consuming thing.

Then Nehemiah came on the scene, a newcomer to the city. No one knew him, and no one shared his passion for rebuilding the walls. But before he had been there a week, he had a full crew signed up to work on those walls.

How did he do it? What quality about this man allowed him to so inspire the people? As we saw in the previous chapter, Nehemiah was a Spirit-filled man, and that was certainly a key. But there's more about Nehemiah's character that equipped him to be the kind of leader who could get the people moving and get those walls up.

Nehemiah had heart. He was a man of passion, a man of compassion, a man of deep emotion. He cared. And he wasn't afraid to let it show.

Go back with me briefly to Nehemiah 1. Remember when Nehemiah first heard the report that the walls of the city were broken down? What was his immediate response?

"So it was, when I heard these words, that I sat down and wept, and mourned for many days; I was fasting and praying before the God of heaven" (1:4). Here was a man who let his emotions get stirred. A great baptism of sorrow got moving inside him, and it transformed him from the inside out.

We've seen that Nehemiah's decision to build the walls was not a thing he entered into lightly. He spent months in prayer, seeking God's will, pleading for God's power, and planning what his course of action would be. During those months of prayer, all the time he was on his knees, Nehemiah's soul was being broken by waves of sorrow and deep emotion that were flowing through him.

Nehemiah's emotional involvement is admittedly a little difficult to conceive of in contemporary terms. We live in a tearless society. Compassion runs low. We rarely weep. We are desensitized to reality, partly because we have been conditioned by television not to believe it, or to see evil as ordinary. We watch murder and violence every night on the little boxes in our living rooms, and we are used to it. We sit with TV dinners, watching the news reports of worldwide hunger, followed by commercials for gourmet catfood, and we don't take anything seriously.

The closest thing we see to compassion is manufactured by the entertainment industry. Someone comes up with an idea to solve the hunger problem: have a televised rock concert and ask for donations. So instead of involvement, we get more entertainment. And it's nothing more than opportunism disguised as humanitarianism. The rock stars get free nationwide exposure, adulation from the masses, and a few thousand more record sales. The money goes to pay salaries, television bills, and finally, whatever is left goes to the starving people. No one weeps, few really sacrifice, and little is done to solve the problem of starvation.

Can you imagine Nehemiah's setting up a concert in Shushan to raise money for the wall? I can't. He wasn't a promoter; he was a champion. He wasn't a publicist; he was a problem solver. He didn't just sit in his easy chair, shake his head, click his tongue, and say, "Somebody ought to do something about that!" He became the somebody who did it.

Crocodile tears are cheap. It's easy to express a superfluous concern, phone in a donation, and then get on with enjoying the concert. But that's a long way away from real compassion.

Nehemiah got involved. He became an activist, but not

in the modern sense of someone who carries protest plac-
ards and marches around. He was a *real* activist, someone
who rolled up his sleeves and jumped into the most difficult part of the task.

The best leaders are always people who get involved.
General Douglas MacArthur, who fought alongside his
men on Corregidor at the outset of World War II, was
personally humiliated when orders from Washington
forced him to leave the battle there and secretly flee the
Philippines. He felt he was betraying his own men and the
Philippino people. He left with the solemn promise, "I
shall return!"

Those words became the battle cry of the Philippine
nation during the years of oppression under the Japanese.
Philippinos were so certain MacArthur *would* return that
they painted his words on walls and fences—even on enemy tanks—all over the islands.

And General MacArthur *did* return. He spent years directing the Allied war effort from Australia, planning a
strategy that would take him back through the Philippines so that he could personally oversee the liberation of
the islands. When the tide of the war turned and the Allied
navy began sailing north again, General MacArthur was
there. During the invasion of the Philippines, MacArthur
personally led the forces that stormed the beaches. He was
so intent on being at the heart of the battle that several
times his men had to plead with him to move to a safer
location, lest he be an easy target. He wasn't afraid to be
involved, even though it might cost him his life. Nothing
meant more to him than his promise to the Philippino
people.

Those who get involved are always people who have heart. God loves to use a person who cares deeply about what matters to Him. I've known many men and women of God in my lifetime, and I've noticed that a common characteristic they all share is that they are people of deep emotion. They're not afraid to cry. They're not afraid to get angry. They're not afraid to laugh. They're not afraid to love and let it show. They are without exception people of great compassion and deep feeling for the individuals they minister to and labor alongside. Just like Nehemiah.

Nehemiah Cared about the Wall

It's interesting to observe what motivates people. I've known people in churches who enjoy sitting on the sidelines. They won't join the choir, come to prayer meetings, do any visitation, or teach Sunday school. Church is a spectator sport for them—until there's a controversy. Then they are usually the first ones to join the fracas, and they'll work as hard as they can for a church split. They'll criticize the pastor, the pastor's wife, the choir, the Sunday school, the prayer meetings, and everything else in which they were always too lazy to participate. They're like Sanballat and Tobiah—negatively motivated. They want only to tear down, not to build up.

Then there are people like the Israelites who helped Nehemiah build the wall. They'll join up when they see something happening, but they're not the ones to make things happen. They are motivated by activity, not by needs.

Thank God for the people like Nehemiah. They're the

ones who see a need and know that *they* must make something happen.

Nehemiah was motivated by a broken-down wall he had never even seen. Other men said it was a disgrace; only Nehemiah really cared enough to do something about it. This was not shallow feeling, but emotion that emanated from his soul. It was part of what made him stand out as a champion.

Why did Nehemiah care so deeply about the wall? Because the wall was a symbol of the city. As long as the walls were broken down, the city was indefensible. There was no privacy. There was no security. The people could be killed by night. Thieves and enemies could come and go at any time. And God's people were living in fear.

Nehemiah, like any good Israelite, loved Jerusalem. It was God's own city. The Temple was there. It was the center of religious life, the place to which pilgrims would come to offer sacrifices and worship God.

Even though he had never seen Jerusalem, Nehemiah loved it as his home. He couldn't bear to think of its walls as piles of rubble. He had to *do* something about it.

Nehemiah Cared about the People

Nehemiah also cared about the people of the city. He came to Jerusalem to help them build the wall, not to goad them into doing it. He was their fellow-worker, not their boss. He rolled up his sleeves and pitched in with them, and he stayed through it even when the going got tough.

Nehemiah 3 isn't the most exciting reading in the Bible. It consists entirely of Nehemiah's chronicle of the names and addresses of those who worked on the wall and where they worked. It's interesting to me that he took the time to record such details. It is also significant that he knew the names of all his co-workers and was familiar with their work firsthand. This is the record of a leader who cared deeply about his people.

In our society, it is not uncommon for a person to live in the same place for years without ever meeting his neighbors. Contemporary humanism says, "Look out for number one." People are conditioned to be selfish, to be chiefly concerned with themselves, not others' needs.

In 1964, a New York woman, Catherine Genovese, was returning home from work when she was attacked by a man with a knife. The attack took place on the street, and at least thirty-eight New Yorkers saw the whole thing. Ignoring the woman's pleas for help, every one of the witnesses turned away, not wanting to get involved. Even though the attack lasted almost twenty minutes, no one came to help, and no one even called the police. Catherine Genovese was brutally murdered while all those people passively watched.

Her case drew a lot of media attention. The world feigned outrage, and everyone expressed horror that such an incident should happen. But in the years since then, the same thing has happened again and again in New York, Chicago, Los Angeles, and even smaller cities. Incidents like that don't get much publicity any more. The rare cases where someone *does* get involved are what make the news now.

Sadly, our society has traded compassion for self-indulgence. We see it reflected in the divorce rate, the crime rate, opinion polls, and every indicator of the current mood of the world. We don't know how to care.

Don't misunderstand Nehemiah's deep emotion. It wasn't wishy-washy. It wasn't showy but shallow emotion. It wasn't even always positive. Nehemiah 5 shows another side of this man's emotion.

He Cared about God's Glory

These were tough times for the people of Israel. Food was scarce, and people had mortgaged their lands to pay taxes. The mortgage rates were so high that people were even selling their children into slavery to pay what they owed.

Nehemiah's reaction when he heard of it is understandable: "I became very angry when I heard their outcry and these words" (5:6). He was upset! He rebuked the noblemen who were charging high interest and demanded that they stop. And they did.

Nehemiah was capable of righteous indignation, because he cared deeply about the glory of God. He was incensed when he observed some breach of righteousness, and he could not be passive.

Jump with me to the final chapter of Nehemiah. This passage took place after Nehemiah had completed the wall and life had pretty much returned to normal in Jerusalem. The entire chapter describes Nehemiah's battle against the encroachment of lethargy, spiritual apathy, and compromise once again. Look at verses 23–25 of chapter 13:

> In those days I also saw Jews who had married women of Ashdod, Ammon, and Moab. And half of their children spoke the language of Ashdod, and could not speak the language of Judah, but spoke according to the language of one or the other people. So I contended with them and cursed them, struck some of them and pulled out their hair, and made them swear by God, saying, "You shall not give your daughters as wives to their sons, nor take their daughters for your sons or yourselves."

The mental image of that scene makes me smile. Nehemiah was so zealous for the glory of God that he wasn't afraid to confront those living in sin. He even got into a fight over it.

"So I contended with them and cursed them, struck some of them and pulled out their hair." This occurred several years after Nehemiah had begun his work on the wall, and he wasn't a young man any more. Yet here he was, fighting with his fists, tearing out hair, ever zealous for the glory of God.

Note an important distinction between carnal anger and righteous indignation: truly righteous indignation has nothing to do with personal offenses against us. It is anger stirred by flagrant sin against God. Its goal is never retribution or vengeance, but repentance.

As we study Nehemiah's story, you'll notice that he faced much personal opposition, especially from those two worthless characters, Sanballat and Tobiah. Nehemiah had plenty of opportunities to get angry with them. He must have been tempted many times to hit them and pull out their hair.

But he never did that. You don't see him getting into fistfights with them, or even answering their barbed comments about him. Why? Because personal opposition was not what stirred his anger. Flagrant unrighteousness and compromise did, but not insults and mockery.

Here's where we get a glimpse of the true depth of Nehemiah's character. He knew that the wrath of man doesn't bring about the righteousness of God (see James 1:20). He had a temper, but he controlled it when he needed to. He allowed himself to get angry only when he saw God's holiness being publicly challenged.

Jesus was like that, too. He wasn't always meek and mild. He got angry when He saw the Temple being defiled. Yet there was no contradiction in His character. He was the most compassionate person who ever lived. He would weep over the multitudes, who were like sheep without a shepherd. He could stand toe to toe with the Pharisees and quietly answer any challenge they put to Him. They could hurl their insults and accusations against Him, and He kept His peace. But when He observed His Father's house being made into a thieves' market, He made a whip and drove them out!

There *is* a place for righteous anger that grows out of a zeal for God's glory. I get angry when I see Christians compromise. I get angry when I see some television preachers making merchandise of the gospel. I get angry when I hear false teachers spouting lies.

It's wrong *not* to get angry at things like that. Positive thinking isn't always the answer. We're supposed to be zealous about God's glory. We should feel deeply about His righteousness. It's good to share God's hatred of sin. That's part of true compassion.

A person who ignores sin and compromise doesn't really care. One who sincerely loves people is like a watchman on the wall, loudly giving the signal when sin and danger are approaching. That was Jesus' whole point in Matthew 18:15–17, where He taught us how to confront sin lovingly, with the aim of restoring a sinning brother to fellowship. It's the natural activity of one who really cares.

Nehemiah would never have succeeded on the wall if he had failed to care. It is this quality of compassion and fervor that makes his character shine so brightly. It's also what gave him the ability to plan, organize, and execute the work on the wall.

What ministry has God given you to do? Do you really care about it? Do you care about the people to whom you are ministering? Do you freely show that you care? Do you weep with those who weep, and mourn with those who mourn? If not, you're not ministering with real effectiveness.

There is one drawback to really caring: it makes you vulnerable. That's why I have so much respect for Nehemiah. Because he cared so much about the people and the job he was doing, he must have really felt the sting of his enemies' verbal onslaughts. It must have hurt him deeply to hear them mock him, laugh at the job he was doing, and tell him he was going to be a failure.

He had committed his life to this task, and his reputation with both the people and the king was on the line. I don't think his reputation was that important to Nehemiah, but because he was a man of deep feeling, I'm sure all the mockery and laughter must have made an impression.

Sanballat and Tobiah were exactly the opposite of Nehemiah. He cared deeply for the people of the city and the wall. Sanballat and Tobiah hated the people and the wall just as fervently. Scripture tells us that "they were deeply disturbed that a man had come to seek the well-being of the children of Israel" (2:10). There are always people like that. No matter what God calls you to do, if you really care about the people and the task, you will encounter someone who feels just as deeply as you, but holds an opposing view.

I've ministered all over the world, and it's the same everywhere I have ever been. Wherever Christians gather to do the work of God, Satan will have his workers there to oppose it. I've confronted demon-possessed people, drunken hecklers, organized crime lords, and even religious professionals who hate the gospel. The more effective the work of the Lord is, the more loudly the enemy's hordes will scream their opposition.

God's choice servants have always had their antagonists. It was no different for Nehemiah, and it won't be different for you. The more you care, the more it will hurt, but you must care deeply if God is to use you as He used Nehemiah.

The blessing of it is that like Nehemiah, we have God's promise of ultimate victory if we are faithful. There will come a day—maybe in your lifetime, maybe when you stand before His throne in eternity—when you will look around at what God has wrought through your faithful labor, and you will know it was worth it all.

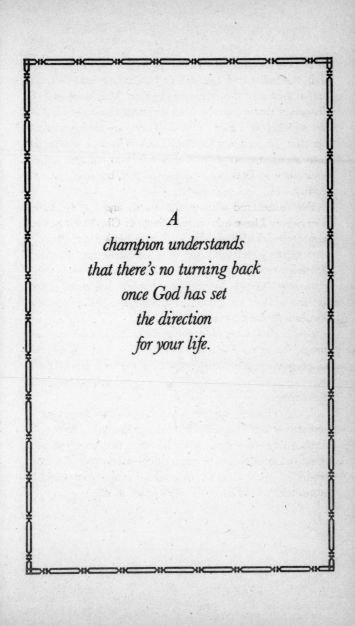

A
champion understands
that there's no turning back
once God has set
the direction
for your life.

6

A Single-Minded Man

*F*rom Shushan to Jerusalem was a three-month-long journey in Nehemiah's day. It wasn't an easy one, either. There was nothing but hundreds of miles of desert. The sun was hot, and the going was slow. Burning in Nehemiah's heart was his passion to build those walls. That's all he had thought about for months, and the long journey must have provided him with more opportunities to pray about his task and plan how he would take it on.

When Nehemiah made the commitment to go to Jerusalem and build the walls, he was making a monumental decision. Perhaps he knew it would be the biggest decision of his life. However, I don't think he realized at that time how far-reaching the effects of it would be. It would drastically alter the course of his life and ultimately earn him a prominent place in the Old Testament record.

I'm convinced that would not have made any difference to Nehemiah. He was not on a quest for fame. Note that Nehemiah did not go to Jerusalem with a lot of fanfare about why he was there. He had the king's own permission and blessing for his expedition, but he didn't announce it when he showed up. In fact, he didn't tell anyone why he was there.

How different that is from modern-day "prophets" who, like the Pharisees of Jesus' day, love to sound a trumpet before them! It's the recognition of men they seek—fame, money, and worldly honor—not the glory of God. Watch out for any person or religious organization that emphasizes marketing above ministry, puts personality before integrity, or focuses on public relations more than divine truth. That wasn't the way of any of the biblical prophets, least of all Nehemiah. He seemed actually to want to *avoid* attention.

Nehemiah wasn't the least bit interested in justifying himself in the eyes of men. Even when Sanballat and Tobiah accused him of rebellion against the king (see 2:19), he didn't bother to try to refute their accusation. He had papers to prove that he wasn't a rebel, but he didn't use them to answer his critics. He was concerned with God's work, not with men's opinions.

It was as if he had set his face steadfastly in the direction he wanted to go, and nothing was going to deter him from it. He wasn't going to get caught up in arguments or incidentals. He wasn't going to waste time trying to justify his mission. He didn't need the approval of admiring throngs, and he didn't even care if anyone knew what he was there to do. He had a job to do, and he was going to do it in his own way and in his own time.

Nehemiah was a single-minded man. Having made up his mind what he wanted to do, he didn't need any other incentive. And he was not about to let anything or anyone deter him.

Some people call that stubbornness, and there is a sense in which it is. But it's the good kind of stubbornness, the kind David wrote of when he penned these words: "I have set the LORD always before me; because He is at my right hand I shall not be moved" (Psa. 16:8).

That's a holy stubbornness. It's the kind of determination we all need to have. It is the opposite of what James wrote about when he spoke of "a double-minded man, unstable in all his ways" (James 1:8).

There was nothing unstable about Nehemiah. From the time he first heard the report about the ravaged city walls, he knew what needed to be done. For him, there was no turning back. There would be no excuses, no hesitation, and no compromise. He was going to rebuild those walls.

No Turning Back

Nehemiah had first demonstrated just how determined he was when he appeared before King Artaxerxes to ask permission to go to Jerusalem. He was risking life and limb by going before the king with a sad countenance.

It was literally the law of the Medes and the Persians that anyone who stood before the king with a cold face, an angry face, or a sad face was to be executed that same day. The king permitted no one in his presence who was not cheerful. That's why Nehemiah said, "Now I had never been sad in his presence before" (2:1).

But being the single-minded man that he was, Nehemiah was unable to put up a front for long, and the day came that he walked into the king's presence with a sad countenance. His attitude was, "If I die, I die." That's commitment! Yet I can't help thinking that Nehemiah half expected the king to respond as he did. Surely he knew that God, having filled his heart with a burden to rebuild those walls, was not going to let him die asking permission.

Note what happened. The king, instead of punishing Nehemiah, asked him, "What do you request?" (2:4). It was an open invitation, a blank check for Nehemiah—and an answer to his months of prayer.

Take a close look at Nehemiah's request to the king. His first response was typical. He paused for prayer. Then he told the king what he wanted: "If it pleases the king, and if your servant has found favor in your sight, I ask that you send me to Judah, to the city of my fathers' tombs, that I may rebuild it" (2:5).

Just in asking that much, Nehemiah was taking a big risk. The king could easily have been angered by the request. After all, he ruled the empire, and Nehemiah was his servant. Who was this cupbearer to become involved in affairs of state? Furthermore, Nehemiah was asking to rebuild the capital city of a conquered nation. The king could easily have accused him of sedition and had him beheaded.

But "the king's heart is in the hand of the LORD, like the rivers of water; He turns it wherever He wishes" (Prov. 21:1). God had orchestrated the entire plan, and He was in control of even the king's response. It shouldn't surprise us that the king gave Nehemiah everything he asked for and more. He gave him time off, letters of reference, timber to build with, and even a small army to protect him on his journey.

None of that would have occurred if Nehemiah had not been totally committed to his calling. If he had been the least bit inclined to turn aside, he would never have risked his life by petitioning the king. But he was a man fully committed to God's will, a single-minded individual who understood that there was no turning back once God has set the direction for your life.

If God has called you to a task, you can be certain He will move heaven and earth to make it possible for you to accomplish whatever He has given you to do. As Nehemiah learned, no obstacle—geographical, cultural, or bureaucratic—is so great that it can halt the work of God. But you have to obey with single-mindedness.

That's not easy to do in the face of overwhelming opposition. I learned this lesson early in my ministry. I was convinced God had called me to preach the gospel to the whole world. As I mentioned in an earlier chapter, I set out from San Francisco on a ship bound for Australia with only twelve dollars in my pocket. I knew God had called me, however, and that He would not let me starve to death.

What I didn't know until I arrived in Sydney was that Australia refused admission to any foreigners who weren't carrying the equivalent of two hundred pounds Australian. I didn't have anywhere near that amount. Before entering the country, I had to fill out a declaration form, and one of the questions it asked was how much money I was carrying. I left that question blank.

I remember the day vividly. My stomach sank as I

watched customs officials refuse entry to the young man in front of me. He had only seventy-five dollars. I knew in my heart that God had not brought me that far only to be refused entry, but I also knew He would have to work a miracle to get me in. It was a test of my resolve, but I was single-mindedly determined to do God's will. I knew that meant I couldn't lie to the customs officer, and I couldn't try to bluff my way through. I decided to let them know how determined I was. Meanwhile, I prayed that God would open the authorities' hearts.

The officer looked up from my declaration form and said, "You've left one question unanswered. How much money do you have on you?" He had a pen out to write the amount.

"I don't have much money," I answered.

"I see you're a minister," he said. "Where do you plan to go from here?"

"I'm on my way around the world to preach," I told him with a boldness I didn't realize I possessed. "I'll be going on to Java, China, Korea, Manchuria, Japan, Europe, and then back to America. God has called me to preach the gospel all over the world, and I know He'll provide for my needs."

The officer spoke briefly with his superior, and they let me into the country! To this day, I don't know why they decided to circumvent their normal policy for me, but I believe that if I had been the least bit hesitant, if I had wavered at all on the question of whether I really believed God had sent me to this place, they would have turned me away as they did the young man in front of me. But as far as I was concerned, there was no turning back. And God honored my faith.

No Excuses

One of the most remarkable aspects of Nehemiah's character is that he was a man who made no excuses. It would have been easy for him to ease off, slow down the work on the wall to a more comfortable pace, and blame the delays on circumstances beyond his control. After all, to build the wall, the workmen literally had to dig the boulders out from piles of garbage (see 4:10). The workers' strength was sapped. The city was short on food. And Sanballat and Tobiah confronted Nehemiah with every kind of opposition they could cook up. There were plenty of excuses to slow down—if Nehemiah had been looking for them.

It took a truly single-minded man to persevere in the face of that kind of difficulty. Anyone with the least inclination to ease up or procrastinate would have lost momentum, and the walls may never have been built.

But Nehemiah wasn't trying to avoid the work. He would do whatever needed to be done to finish the job. The lies didn't matter to him. The threats were nothing. The difficulty of the work made no difference. He was there to do a job, and he wasn't looking for any excuses to get out of it.

Most of us would have to admit that we're not always like that. We love to use excuses. We make up excuses for what we do that we shouldn't, and other excuses for what we should do but don't. Excuses are a pathetic way to avoid facing responsibility.

It's amazing how far some people will go to make excuses. No one knows this better than a policeman who gives speeding tickets or an insurance adjuster who must process accident reports. I recently read some humorous samples from actual statements submitted by drivers explaining accidents to their insurance companies. Here are a few of them:

- A pedestrian hit me and went under my car.

- Coming home, I drove into the wrong house and collided with a tree I don't have.

- As I approached the intersection, a stop sign suddenly appeared at a place where no stop sign had ever appeared before. I was unable to avoid the accident.

- The other car attempted to cut in front of me, so I, with my right bumper, removed his left front tail light.

- I pulled away from the side of the road, glanced at my mother-in-law, and headed over the embankment.

- As I reached the intersection, a hedge sprang up obscuring my vision. I did not see the other car.

- The accident occurred when I was attempting to bring my car out of a skid by steering it into the other vehicle.

- An invisible car came out of nowhere and struck my vehicle and vanished.

- The indirect cause of this accident was a little guy in a small car with a big mouth.

- In my attempt to kill a fly, I drove into a telephone pole.

- My car was legally parked as it backed into the other vehicle.

- I was sure the old fellow would make it to the other side of the road when I struck him.

- When I saw I could not avoid the collision, I stepped on the gas and crashed into the other car.

- The telephone pole was approaching fast. I was attempting to swerve out of its path when it struck my front end.

Some of those excuses make us laugh only because we see a bit of ourselves in them. We realize that all our excuses are only thinly veiled deceit, feeble attempts to divert blame from where it really lies—with us. And of course when we stand before God in judgment, there will no excuses.

It's refreshing to see a no-excuses individual like Nehemiah. His single-minded refusal to seek alibis or back down is part of what made him the great champion he was.

No Hesitation

Nehemiah never hesitated to do what he knew God wanted of him, even though it meant that he must go to a place where he had never been, engage in a work he had no experience for, and lead people he had never met.

When he first got to Jerusalem, he was bursting with a desire to get the work under way, but for three days he didn't tell anyone. He wanted to see those walls firsthand, without letting anyone know why he was there. "I arose in the night," he recorded in Nehemiah 2:12–13, "I and a few men with me; I told no one what my God had put in my heart to do at Jerusalem. . . . And I went out by night through the Valley Gate to the Serpent Well and the Refuse Gate, and viewed the walls of Jerusalem." He was so anxious to survey those walls that he didn't sleep at night.

What was he doing in those three initial days? It is certain that he wasn't wavering on his commitment to build the wall. He wasn't trying to make up his mind whether to go through with it. That decision had already been made, and he was not about to turn back. These weren't days of hesitation, they were days of planning. He was surveying the walls, meeting the people, mapping out a plan of attack.

Nehemiah had that quality of decisiveness and determination that is essential to a great leader. In all his story, there is no indication that he ever hesitated or delayed making any important decision, even for a moment. He wasn't impetuous, and he didn't make hasty decisions, but he never delayed, either. He always surveyed the situation, gathered the facts, prayed for wisdom, then acted decisively.

Nehemiah didn't skip the planning stage, but he didn't drag it out. He didn't send the plan through a maze of committees seeking approval, and he didn't use planning as an excuse for delay. He developed a simple plan, and then he immediately put it into effect.

Once he had a workable plan, which in this case took only three days, he immediately set to work putting it into effect. He gathered the people of Jerusalem and gave them a simple pep talk: "You see the distress that we are in, how Jerusalem lies waste, and its gates are burned with fire. Come and let us build the wall of Jerusalem, that we may no longer be a reproach" (2:17).

His decisiveness and sense of urgency were contagious, for once he told the people how God's hand had been good upon him, they said, "Let us rise up and build" (v. 18). They were eager to get started! There was no hesitation in their response. No one said, "Well, as soon as this year's harvest comes in, I'll help." Nobody asked to send the plan back for further study. No one wanted to do cost analyses and get competitive bids. They wanted to get to work! Scripture says they immediately "set their hands to do this good work" (v. 18). In other words, they picked up their tools and got in line to work.

No Compromise

Nehemiah was an uncompromising man. He was determined to do the job right, without compromise. Having made a plan, he did not modify it to suit the preferences of his critics. And his critics were extremely vocal. They mocked him, they publicly held him up to scorn, they accused him of wrong motives, and they made fun of his plan.

Nothing they did deterred Nehemiah, though. He took his instructions from the Lord, and he didn't need to adapt them to make people happy.

In a later chapter, we'll look closely into this aspect of

Nehemiah's character that enabled him to obey God without compromise. For now, though, I want to point out that to Nehemiah "no compromise" did not mean "no cooperation."

There are Christians today who think that in order to be uncompromising, they must refuse to cooperate with anyone for anything. They fight with other Christians over minor points of preference in doctrine or behavior, and they refuse to have fellowship with anyone who has a different point of view. That's not an uncompromising attitude—it's divisiveness.

Nehemiah would not compromise, but if he was going to build the wall, he had to cooperate. Such a large task would require armies of men, all working together, side by side. There was no room for division, no place for sectarianism. Each group had to build its section of the wall in accordance with what everyone else was doing. One renegade bricklayer could destroy the whole effort.

Cooperation without compromise. It's a difficult tightrope to walk. But nothing about building a broken-down city wall is easy.

James wrote, "He who doubts is like a wave of the sea driven and tossed by the wind. For let not that man suppose that he will receive anything from the Lord; he is a double-minded man, unstable in all his ways" (James 1:6–8).

"Let not that man suppose that he will receive anything from the Lord." Those are harsh words, aren't they? But perhaps they explain why some of our prayers seem to go unanswered. God wants us to be men and women of strong faith, single-minded like Nehemiah, stable in all our ways.

That means there's no room for excuses, no place for hesitation, and no possibility for compromise. A builder for God must build according to God's plan, brick by brick, with unadulterated materials, methods, and motives. The wall we're putting up is too important to do haphazardly.

Evaluate the situation. Make a plan. Recruit some help. But don't hold back when the time comes to roll up your sleeves and start building the wall.

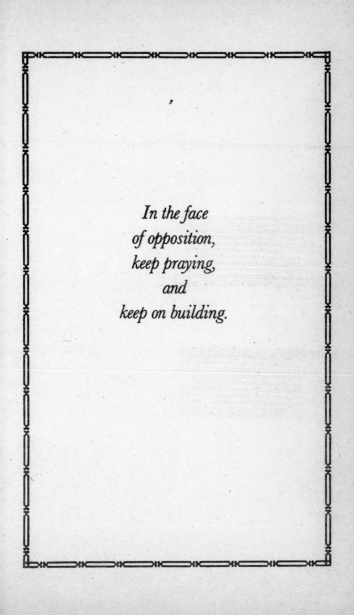

In the face
of opposition,
keep praying,
and
keep on building.

7

Holding Up Under Attack

Nehemiah had been in Jerusalem for less than a week when he learned a very important lesson: nothing that is done for the Lord will be done without opposition. Wherever God's people are doing a great work, Satan will have his minions there to thwart it. Every great man of God in Scripture had his enemies, and Jesus Himself faced the severest opposition of all.

That shouldn't surprise us. Satan is shrewd enough not to waste his efforts where there is no threat to his program. But you can be sure that wherever something worthwhile in the Kingdom is going on, Satan will launch an all-out effort to put a stop to it.

Almost before Nehemiah had unpacked his bags from the long journey, Sanballat and Tobiah confronted him. Scripture tells us that "they were deeply disturbed" that someone had come to do something good for the people of Israel (Neh. 2:10).

Sanballat was furious that someone would come to Jerusalem to do something for the Jews! He was the governor of Samaria, and that made him very important around Jerusalem. This wicked Gentile ruler liked to wring shows of respect out of the downtrodden Jews. It made him feel important to make them bow and scrape before him, and he didn't want anyone coming in to make things better for them. A man like Nehemiah was a great threat to Sanballat, because if Nehemiah succeeded, all the people would have a new sense of self-worth. Jerusalem would be a real city, defensible, self-sufficient, with no need to come to Sanballat for favors. He would no longer be able to get men to cower at his presence. So a lot was at stake for this evil man.

Tobiah was also a corrupt official, a ruler of some sort from the nearby Ammonite nation. Like Sanballat, he was an evil Gentile intruder who loved to prey on the people of the broken city. Together, they were like scavenger birds, plucking the eyes out of a not-yet-dead victim, trying to hasten the demise of the city while stuffing themselves with whatever morsels they could get.

Theirs was a devilish hatred, for it extended beyond the Jewish nation to the God the people of Jerusalem worshiped. Sanballat and Tobiah's very presence aggravated the condition that had motivated Nehemiah from the beginning: God's glory was at stake, and the testimony of Israel was void as long as men like these wicked rulers had their way in a defenseless Jerusalem. It was their influence and their diabolical domination that Nehemiah had come to crush.

You can easily understand why these two men were so quick to rise up against the work on the walls. I'm sure Nehemiah was not at all shocked to see them. He knew in his heart that they would oppose him, and perhaps that's why he wanted to raise the walls as quickly as possible—to take them by surprise, before they had a chance to act decisively.

Nehemiah was wise to their tactics. Take a lesson from him: the enemy should never be able to blind side us. The apostle Paul wrote to the Corinthians, "We are not ignorant of his devices" (2 Cor. 2:11). It's true. We know how Satan works. We're familiar with his strategies. His game plan is the same as it has always been.

And the opposition Satan threw up against Nehemiah was nothing new. He used Sanballat and Tobiah to exercise all his favorite weapons, one after the other. The attack against Nehemiah bears a lot of resemblance to Satan's attack against Adam and Eve, which was not that different from his attack against Job, which was similar to his attack against Jesus in the wilderness, which is the very same way he attacks us all. He doesn't have any new tricks up his sleeve; he doesn't need them. His strategies are too often horribly effective.

Ridicule

The first stage of Satan's attack was ridicule. Sanballat and Tobiah eagerly attacked Nehemiah's plan, even while he was introducing it to the people. Nehemiah said that when they heard his plan to build the wall, "*they laughed us to scorn* and despised us, and said, 'What is this thing that you are doing? Will you rebel against the king?'" (2:19, emphasis added).

They didn't really care about whether Nehemiah was rebelling against the king. If that had been a legitimate concern, Nehemiah had papers from the king endorsing his mission. His equipment came from the king. The trowels he was using to spread the mortar came from the king. His provisions came from the king. The timber he was using for support and scaffolding had been cut according to the king's orders. Nehemiah and his crew weren't the ones rebelling against the king, Sanballat and Tobiah were.

These evil men were really concerned about their own little dominions. This was an attempt at intimidation by ridicule. No one before Nehemiah had ever failed to truckle to them, and perhaps they thought their little barbs would put an end to the whole thing there and then. But they didn't know whom they were really up against.

Nehemiah didn't appeal to the king as his defense, though he could have. He correctly saw beyond the king of Persia and knew that the God of heaven was the One directing this whole project. Nehemiah understood that Sanballat's rebellion was ultimately against God, too, so he appealed to Jehovah Himself as the authority for this mission: "The God of heaven Himself will prosper us; therefore we His servants will arise and build, but you have no heritage or right or memorial in Jerusalem" (2:20).

In modern language, "Get out of town! We take our orders from the Lord, not from the likes of you."

The next time we see Sanballat, the wall was under construction, the work was progressing well, and he was angrier than ever about it. He had gone beyond being furious; now he was throwing a fit. Scripture says he was "very indignant" (4:1). That means he "blew his stack!"

Furthermore, Sanballat had brought in the Samarian army. Perhaps he thought a little show of force would cause these people to sit up and take notice.

Imagine the effect of that to the men working on the wall. They were just beginning to make progress when they heard the mocking voice of their long-time oppressor Sanballat down below. They turned and looked, and there was this man who had dominated them for so long, standing there with a group of his thugs. Nehemiah 4:1–2 describes the scene. Sanballat was hopping mad and still using mockery as his weapon:

> But it so happened, when Sanballat heard that we were rebuilding the wall, that he was furious and very indignant, and mocked the Jews. And he spoke before his brethren and the army of Samaria, and said, "What are these feeble Jews doing? Will they fortify themselves? . . . Will they complete it in a day? Will they revive the stones from the heaps of rubbish—stones that are burned?"

You can almost see him, pacing up and down in front of the wall, spouting forth as loudly and as bitterly as he knew how. His sidekick Tobiah was even more vicious: "Now Tobiah the Ammonite was beside him, and he said, 'Whatever they build, if even a fox goes up on it, he will break down their stone wall'" (v. 3).

This was psychological warfare. Sanballat and Tobiah were playing mind games with the workmen building the wall, attacking their faith in the legitimacy of what they were doing. "You don't amount to anything! You're just digging rocks out of the garbage pile. And that little wall you're building—well, you'd better hope a fox doesn't try to climb up it! Because if he does, he's liable to knock the whole thing down!" You can almost hear the coarse laughter of the army standing around.

Nehemiah's heart must have sunk. Surely *he* wasn't discouraged, but being a great leader, he was anxious that his crew not be demoralized by this verbal onslaught.

I know firsthand what he was up against. In one city where I ministered, the gamblers on Main Street laid odds against our completing a church building. They gambled on it—bet money that we would not be able to finish the building! They said that because the payments were so high, we would lose the building, and they voiced it around town that they were taking bets against us.

I know how Nehemiah felt. I was confident that God was in that building project and that we would ultimately be victorious (and I was right). But in the meantime, I had the difficult task of trying to keep the people's morale up in the face of ruthless mockery. When the building was complete and we burned the mortgage, the odds makers were strangely silent.

What they didn't realize—and what Nehemiah's detractors didn't understand—was that they were not mocking the work of men, but of God. Notice again Tobiah's words in verse 3: "If even a fox goes up on it, he will break down their stone wall." The point that Tobiah missed, and the issue that would ultimately destroy him, was that this was not *their* stone wall. This was *God's* wall. The plan to build it was His plan. The people building it were His people. The energy to do the work was His power.

The success or failure of this project depended on the faithfulness of the builders and the power of God, not on the cooperation of Sanballat and Tobiah. They could threaten, mock, and cajole all they liked, but they could do nothing to stop this work of the Lord. As long as His people were trusting Him and working in His power, it was futile to oppose.

That doesn't mean, however, that Nehemiah did not need to take their challenge seriously. If the people of God became discouraged, turned away from the work, lost faith, or became demoralized, the work might stall. He could not allow his builders to be swayed by the enemies' mockery.

How did Nehemiah face this challenge? He did what he always did in a difficult situation. He prayed. "Hear, O our God, for we are despised; turn their reproach on their own heads, and give them as plunder to a land of captivity! Do not cover their iniquity, and do not let their sin be blotted out from before You; for they have provoked You to anger before the builders" (4:4–5).

Not a pretty prayer, is it? But note that Nehemiah was not angry because of a personal attack on himself. He didn't say, "for they have provoked *me*," but "they have provoked You to anger *before the builders*." He was concerned about two things: the Lord's honor and the workmen's morale.

This was not a "Forgive them for they know not what they do" kind of prayer. Sanballat and Tobiah *did* know exactly what they were doing. They were attacking the God of Israel and mocking Him. They had seen those walls lie in ruins for years, and perhaps they really thought that Jehovah didn't have the power to raise them up. Nehemiah wanted them punished, not because they had challenged him, but because they had attacked God and demoralized the people.

The very next verse after Nehemiah's prayer is perhaps the most significant statement in this entire account: "So we built the wall" (v. 6). They just kept right on working. And that was the best response Nehemiah could have given Sanballat and Tobiah. No verbal retaliation. No volley of threats. No response at all, except to keep right on putting stones in their place.

Nothing deflates ridicule as quickly as persistence. Sanballat's tirade just dropped among the garbage in the ruins of the old wall. Nobody responded. Nobody paid attention. They simply kept on building, and God was glorified. Nehemiah recorded, "And the entire wall was joined together up to half its height, for the people had a mind to work" (4:6).

Praise the Lord, and pass a trowel full of mortar!

Violence

But the opposition wasn't finished. Satan was about to fire his second salvo. If ridicule and mockery had no effect, he would try the threat of physical violence. Nehemiah 4:7-8 describes it:

> Now it happened, when Sanballat, Tobiah, the
> Arabs, the Ammonites, and the Ashdodites heard
> that the walls of Jerusalem were being restored and
> the gaps were beginning to be closed, that they be-
> came very angry, and all of them conspired together
> to come and attack Jerusalem and create confusion.

The walls were half built. That must have frightened
Sanballat and Tobiah. These builders were actually making progress!

From Nehemiah's perspective, it had to be the worst
possible time for his enemies to launch a full-scale physical
attack. The work on the wall was getting harder. The further along they got, the deeper they had to dig to get the
old wall stones out of the piles of rubbish. And the higher
the walls grew, the more effort it took to get the large boulders into position.

His response once again was to pray and keep on working. "Nevertheless we made our prayer to our God, and
because of them we set a watch against them day and
night" (v. 9). Notice that they put feet to their prayers
and took the action of setting watchmen on the wall. Nehemiah loaded the wall with as many people to stand
guard as he could recruit. It was a good tactic—reverse
intimidation—and it worked. Verses 13–15 describe what
happened:

> Therefore I positioned men behind the lower parts of
> the wall, at the openings; and I set the people ac-
> cording to their families, with their swords, their
> spears, and their bows. And I looked, and arose and

said to the nobles, to the leaders, and to the rest of the people, "Do not be afraid of them. Remember the Lord, great and awesome, and fight for your brethren, your sons, your daughters, your wives, and your houses." And it happened, when our enemies heard that it was known to us, and that God had brought their counsel to nothing, that all of us returned to the wall, everyone to his work.

Nehemiah even mobilized the women and the children to stand on the wall with weapons and watch around the clock for any surprise attacks. When Sanballat and Tobiah and their hordes heard they had lost the element of surprise, they scrapped their plans for attack.

Discouragement

A subtler danger was lurking to hinder the work. Satan had already launched another attack—this time from within. Discouragement threatened to hamper the builders. Some messengers from the tribe of Judah came to Nehemiah with this word: "The strength of the laborers is failing, and there is so much rubbish that we are not able to build the wall" (4:10).

I'm amazed at how frequently men of God who win great victories against the enemy and for the Kingdom subsequently cave in to the threat of discouragement. Satan knows that if he can't divert our attention with an external threat, he can still nail us with discouragement, even while we're on the threshold of total victory.

It happened to Elijah that way. First Kings 18 describes

his great battle with the prophets of Baal. There, this one man stood against 450 false prophets and challenged them to call down fire out of heaven. His life was in danger; he had been sought by King Ahab for years because of the drought he had brought upon the land. Now, in a head-to-head confrontation, he stood boldly against an entire army of false prophets and defeated them. Every one of those false prophets died by the sword that afternoon as God miraculously gave Elijah the victory.

But in the very next chapter, we see an amazing sight. Here was Elijah, huddled under a tree, crying out to God to take his life, because he was afraid to die at the hands of a woman. Was this the same man? Yes, but he fell victim to an attack of discouragement. Fearful, hungry, and exhausted from a long journey on foot, he was a prime victim for one of Satan's internal attacks.

From our human vantage point, it would seem that the biggest threat to Nehemiah's efforts was the army of men assembling to come down on them. But in reality it was this encroaching defeatism that posed the greater danger. An enemy you can see is easier to defend against than one that comes invisibly from within the ranks.

Nehemiah 5:1-5 continues the account of Satan's relentless attack of discouragement:

> And there was a great outcry of the people and their wives against their Jewish brethren. For there were those who said, "We, our sons, and our daughters are many; therefore let us get grain for them, that we may eat and live." There were also some who said, "We have mortgaged our lands and vineyards and

houses, that we might buy grain because of the famine." There were also those who said, "We have borrowed money for the king's tax on our lands and vineyards. Yet now our flesh is as the flesh of our brethren, our children as their children; and indeed we are forcing our sons and our daughters to be slaves, and some of our daughters are brought into slavery already. It is not in our power to redeem them, for other men have our lands and vineyards."

All of that came as news to Nehemiah. He had no idea that the money-lenders were charging such high interest rates that it oppressed the people. That was called *usury*, and it was strictly forbidden by Jewish law (see Exod. 22:25).

Nehemiah appealed to their sense of righteousness, and to their patriotism. These were their fellow countrymen, and to oppress them was to oppress the nation. "Please, let *us* stop this usury! Restore now to them, even this day, their lands, their vineyards, their olive groves, and their houses, also the hundredth part of the money and the grain, the new wine and the oil, that you have charged them" (5:10–11, emphasis added).

A pretty big request, right? But notice the word *us*. Nehemiah was carefully building a sense of national identity, a feeling of community, among the inhabitants of Jerusalem. That was the whole point of the wall. As long as the walls were down, they weren't really a city. With the walls up, they could begin to have some civic pride. But not if they were all the while devouring one another.

So Nehemiah was saying to the money-lenders, "Look,

what's good for these people is good for the community. And what's good for the community is good for you."

Not only that, but he was appealing to their consciences as well. They knew that what they were doing was unlawful. By exacting usury, they were behaving just like Sanballat and Tobiah. They had no right to oppress their brethren, and they knew it.

"So they said, 'We will restore it, and will require nothing from them; we will do as you say'" (v. 12). Notice from verses 12–13 how Nehemiah then sealed their decision:

> Then I called the priests, and required an oath from them that they would do according to this promise. Then I shook out the fold for my garment and said, "So may God shake out each man from his house, and from his property, who does not perform this promise. Even thus may he be shaken out and emptied." And all the congregation said, "Amen!" and praised the LORD. Then the people did according to this promise.

There you see a wise leader at work. The problem was discouragement. His solution was threefold: first, get the people to obey God's Word. Second, instill a strong sense of unity and fellowship. Finally, confirm it in a public way.

It's harder to be discouraged when you're a part of a team. When you know you're not alone, it's impossible to feel that everyone else is against you. When Elijah plunged into his depression, what did he say? "I alone am left; and they seek to take my life" (1 Kings 19:10). And what message did God give him to undo that defeatism? "Yet I have reserved seven thousand in Israel, all whose knees have not bowed to Baal, and every mouth that has not kissed him" (1 Kings 19:18). You're not alone!

That's why the church is so important in the work of God here on earth. Christians are a body—we're never alone. When you're tempted to be discouraged, remember this: you are only one member of a large body, and when one member hurts, the others hurt with it (cf. 1 Cor. 12:26). You are *not* alone if you're in Christ.

Nehemiah was an amazing man, endued with great wisdom. In the face of both savage opposition from outside and subtle attack from within, many leaders turn sour. Not Nehemiah. He kept praying, and he kept building.

Those are always the right responses to opposition, aren't they? It's never right to retaliate. It's never right to return evil for evil. If we give up, the enemy has won the battle. And if we become bitter, it's as if we have joined his side.

But it is always right to seek refuge in the Lord. His promise is sure: "No weapon formed against you shall prosper, and every tongue which rises against you in judgment you shall condemn. This is the heritage of the servants of the LORD, and their righteousness is from Me, says the LORD" (Isa. 54:17).

Above all, it's always right to keep building. No mockery, no slander, no attack of the enemy can tear down the edifice that we're working with God to build.

We can't always be sure when or how we might suffer attack, but one thing is certain: we *will* be attacked. Paul wrote to Timothy, "Yes, and all who desire to live godly in Christ Jesus will suffer persecution" (2 Tim. 3:12). It isn't merely a possibility; it's a fact. When we consecrate ourselves to the work of the Lord, Satan dedicates himself to opposing us. We may face ridicule, the threat of violence, discouragement, or all three, but we *will* be subjected to Satan's onslaughts. So don't be discouraged when it happens. Just keep on praying, and keep on building.

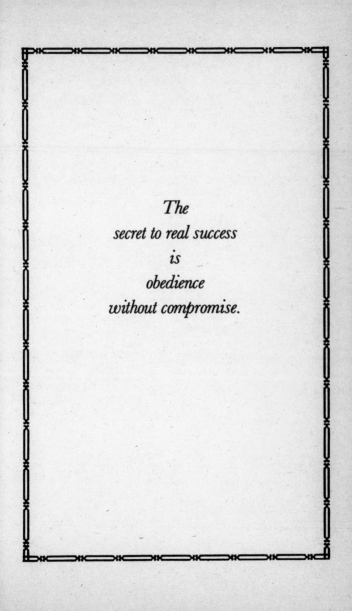

The
secret to real success
is
obedience
without compromise.

8

Resisting the Pressure to Compromise

*N*ehemiah and his army of builders must have been quite a sight to the eyes of Sanballat and the Samarian army. There they were, with trowels in one hand and swords in the other (see 4:17), working side by side at an impossible job—and getting it done.

Sanballat must have realized by now that Nehemiah was working with supernatural assistance.

Having exhausted his supply of direct attacks, Sanballat, a tool in the hands of Satan, moved on to trickery. If he couldn't intimidate Nehemiah into coming down off that wall, perhaps he could get him to compromise.

That is Satan's way every time. You can count on it. When the devil finds someone working for God, if he can't intimidate him, if he can't demoralize him, if he can't subdue him with discouragement, he will try to get him to compromise.

117

Compromise is a peculiar word. The world, by and large, sees compromise as a good thing. Compromise has such a nice feeling to it. You give a little and I'll give a little, and we can overcome our differences through compromise. It's so easy to solve conflicts through compromise. Can compromise really be that bad?

There are times when compromise *is* a good thing. It's not wrong to compromise a matter of preference, to yield ground for the sake of making peace, as long as no matters of good and evil are at stake.

But this is the real issue: although it is seldom wrong to compromise in matters of preference, it is *always* wrong to compromise in matters of principle. There is no need to make peace with the enemies of God. To do so is to become one of them (cf. James 4:4).

The pressure to compromise is strong. The history of Israel is the story of a nation that constantly faced temptation to compromise—and often yielded. The Old Testament records cycle after cycle of compromise, defeat, repentance, victory, apathy, compromise, and so on.

Interestingly, the greatest compromises usually take place on the doorstep of our greatest victories. Satan knows we're most vulnerable when we think we have him licked. "Let him who thinks he stands take heed lest he fall" (1 Cor. 10:12). When you are about to win a great battle, don't throw it away by making peace with the enemy.

World War II began with a compromise that many thought would bring peace with the enemy. Many of us still remember the picture of Neville Chamberlain, the British prime minister, stepping off an airplane in London in 1938, waving a piece of paper that he said guaranteed "peace in our time." Chamberlain had negotiated a pact with Hitler, which he thought would insure that Germany would not wage war against Europe. In return for Hitler's promise not to invade the European nations, Britain and France had ceded Czechoslovakia to Hitler. Their agreement, the infamous Munich Pact, precipitated the most devastating worldwide conflict ever waged.

The Munich Pact was a shameful compromise, and it proved to be one the of the greatest mistakes England has ever made. Hitler showed that he was not a man who could be pacified by compromise. Within days, he launched a murderous campaign against all of Europe, and World War II was underway.

Compromise with evil is the same as defeat. But it is voluntary defeat, a willful yielding to Satan of that which he cannot gain through his evil devices.

Satan cannot be pacified by compromise, and God will not make peace with evil. That first step toward compromise with the enemy is a step down the road to backsliding that can only lead ultimately to terrible defeat and destruction.

Understandably, Satan will offer every incentive to compromise. But again, "we are not ignorant of his devices" (2 Cor. 2:11), and the wise man or woman of God will resist every effort the enemy makes to lure him or her to compromise. Watch how Nehemiah did just that.

An Invitation to Dialogue

The devil's first attempt to allure Nehemiah to compromise was an invitation to dialogue. That is typical of Satan's strategies. After all, we think, is it so wrong to seek communication? Shouldn't we talk over our differences and try to arrive at a resolution?

Not when the conflict is clearly good versus evil. "For what fellowship has righteousness with lawlessness? And what communion has light with darkness? And what accord has Christ with Belial? Or what part has a believer with an unbeliever?" (2 Cor. 6:14–15). No good can ever come from trying to find a point of agreement between good and evil. There is none. And it's always a serious mistake for the children of God to dialogue with the servants of the devil. You just can't be friends with a serpent.

Nehemiah knew that no good thing could come from a meeting with Sanballat and Tobiah. The wall was all but complete; only the gates were left to be hung. Nehemiah was on the threshold of victory. This was no time to try to make peace with the enemy. Nehemiah 6:1–4 describes the scenario:

> Now it happened when Sanballat, Tobiah, Geshem the Arab, and the rest of our enemies heard that I had rebuilt the wall, and that there were no breaks left in it (though at that time I had not hung the doors in the gates), that Sanballat and Geshem sent to me, saying, "Come, let us meet together in one of the villages in the plain of Ono."

But Nehemiah wasn't falling for it:

> But they thought to do me harm. So I sent messengers to them, saying, "I am doing a great work, so that I cannot come down. Why should the work cease while I leave it and go down to you?" But they

sent me this message four times, and I answered
them in the same manner. (6:2–4)

Four times they approached him with an invitation to
talk, and four times he flatly turned them down.

I'm glad that's so clear in Scripture. So often, I fear,
God's people are too eager to meet with the enemy on his
terms. It's easy to justify this kind of compromise by
thinking it's an opportunity to witness, or to believe
wrongly that we're just being open-minded.

Sanballat had all the witness he needed—in the form of
an almost-finished wall. And Nehemiah wasn't interested
in being open-minded. He had a wall to complete. "I am
doing a great work, so that I cannot come down. Why
should the work cease while I leave it and go down to
you?" (v. 3).

Thank God for such a strong stand! Indeed, why *should*
he have come down? His great work was almost done.
Sanballat had done nothing but mock and threaten and
try to stop the building of the wall. What possible righteous reason could he have had to make friends with the
children of God at this point?

There is no need to negotiate with evil, ever. But when
you're winning the battle, Satan will always extend the
invitation. You can count on it.

Extortion

Those first four letters were friendly invitations—or at
least they appeared to be. Nehemiah had turned them
down, perhaps not so graciously. Sanballat was getting

annoyed. No one had ever treated him this way! It was time to play hard ball:

> Then Sanballat sent his servant to me as before, the fifth time, with an open letter in his hand. In it was written: "It is reported among the nations, and Geshem says, that you and the Jews plan to rebel; therefore, according to these rumors, you are rebuilding the wall, that you may be their king. And you have also appointed prophets to proclaim concerning you at Jerusalem, saying, 'There is a king in Judah!' Now these matters will be reported to the king." (6:5–7)

Vicious, slanderous words! But then the punch line: "So come, therefore, and let us take counsel together" (v. 7).

It is significant that this was an open letter. That means it was to be read aloud and sent around to various influential people, so that everyone could hear the accusations against Nehemiah. Sanballat was fueling the rumor mill, trying to incite gossip and slander against Nehemiah so that he would have to divert his energies from work on the wall to the task of trying to clear his name.

This was nothing short of extortion, and it was a clever ploy. If Nehemiah refused the invitation, Sanballat would point to his refusal as an admission that he was guilty of subversion against the king. Rumors of his "rebellion" would reach Shushan, unless he went there to head them off. His other option was to meet with Sanballat, who alone could stop the rumors before they got started. Either way, Nehemiah would be forced to leave the work on the wall at a critical time.

Nehemiah would not yield. A man of unimpeachable discernment, he stood his ground firmly and refused to budge. His responses were beginning to seem predictable: "Then I sent to him, saying, 'No such things as you say are being done, but you invent them in your own heart.' For they all were trying to make us afraid, saying, 'Their hands will be weakened in the work, and it will not be done.' Now therefore, O God, strengthen my hands" (6:8–9).

Did you catch that last phrase? Again, Nehemiah turned to the Lord in prayer in an hour of difficulty. It was the only possible right response. He couldn't waste his effort defending himself, and he wasn't about to yield to Sanballat and go to Ono. Oh, no!

But he could turn to the Lord in prayer. God could do for Nehemiah what he couldn't do for himself: defend his name against a lying tongue, even as far away as the palace at Shushan.

Confusion

Nehemiah's blunt response only fueled Sanballat's fire. If he couldn't entice Nehemiah to compromise, and if he couldn't blackmail him into coming to Ono, perhaps he could sow a little confusion in Nehemiah's camp. Verse 10 tells what happened next:

> Afterward I came to the house of Shemaiah the son of Delaiah, the son of Mehetabeel, who was a secret informer; and he said, "Let us meet together in the house of God, within the temple, and let us close the

doors of the temple, for they are coming to kill you;
indeed, at night they will come to kill you."

Shemaiah was a false prophet, in league with Sanballat
and Tobiah, and his mission was to scare Nehemiah into
disobeying God by giving a false prophecy. He purported
to have a word from the Lord that an assassin was lurking
about who would try to snuff Nehemiah out. Shemaiah,
adding to the drama by asking for a closed-door meeting
in his house, urged Nehemiah to take refuge with him in
the Temple.

Since Nehemiah was determined to appeal always to
his faith in God, Satan would attack him on that basis—
and encourage him to do something that appeared, on the
face of it, to be religious. He would give him incentive to
seek refuge in the Temple.

The phrase "within the temple" comes from a Hebrew
term that referred to the Holy of Holies, the sacred place
within the Temple where only the high priest was allowed
to go, and that only once a year to offer blood. Shemaiah
was proposing something that violated the most basic laws
of God.

Nehemiah wisely saw through the ploy. "And I said,
'Should such a man as I flee? And who is there such as I
who would go into the temple to save his life? I will not go
in!'" (v. 11). His response was fearless. He knew that if he
displayed cowardice at this point, all the men who worked
with him on the wall would be confused. God had pro-
tected him thus far. Why should he run away now?

Nehemiah knew now that Shemaiah was a false
prophet: "Then I perceived that God had not sent him at

all, but that he pronounced this prophecy against me because Tobiah and Sanballat had hired him. For this reason he was hired, that I should be afraid and act that way and sin, so that they might have occasion for an evil report, that they might reproach me" (vv. 12–13). No true prophet would have encouraged him to do something that violated the written Word of God.

Again, Nehemiah prayed for God to take care of the situation: "My God, remember Tobiah and Sanballat, according to these their works, and the prophetess Noadiah and the rest of the prophets who would have made me afraid" (v. 14). And back to work he went.

Subversion

Incredibly, the work on the walls was completed only fifty-two days after the first stone was laid (see 6:15). His work finally finished, Nehemiah let us in on a little secret he knew all along: his enemies had spies in the city. Because of the Jews' intermarriage with the pagan nations, Tobiah had in-laws who lived in Jerusalem and sent him regular updates on Nehemiah's progress.

> Moreover in those days the nobles of Judah sent many letters to Tobiah, and the letters of Tobiah came to them. For many in Judah were pledged to him, because he was the son-in-law of Shechaniah the son of Arah, and his son Jehohanan had married the daughter of Meshullam the son of Berechiah. Also they reported his good deeds before me, and reported my words to him. And Tobiah sent letters to frighten me. (6:17–19)

It certainly would have put me in fear to know that the enemy had some players on my team. It was just one more battle Nehemiah had to fight—the subversion of traitors within the camp.

That is Satan's trump card. He is a master at making his evil workers seem like the good guys. If he can't get us to compromise with overt evil, perhaps he can lure us by making evil look good.

Paul wrote of this phenomenon in 2 Corinthians 11:13–15: "Such are false apostles, deceitful workers, transforming themselves into apostles of Christ. And no wonder! For Satan himself transforms himself into an angel of light. Therefore it is no great thing if his ministers also transform themselves into ministers of righteousness." If the devil can't get us to Ono, he will infiltrate the ranks. And it takes a person of keen discernment to realize that not everyone is what he appears to be. There are many who claim to be on the Lord's side who are really fighting for the devil.

All the way down the line, Nehemiah resisted the pressure to compromise. He overcame flattery, extortion, confusion, intimidation, and deception, all because he knew that you don't compromise with the enemy on the eve of great victory.

The wall was complete. The victory was won. And Nehemiah had done it without yielding one inch of ground to the enemy.

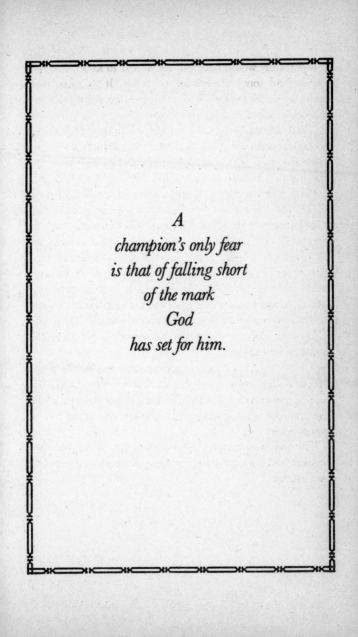

*A
champion's only fear
is that of falling short
of the mark
God
has set for him.*

9

Cowardice and Courage

Sanballat, Tobiah, and their evil cohorts were typical bullies. Bullies are people who try to mask their cowardice and pass it off as courage. All their threats and fiery rhetoric were just cloaking the fact that in their hearts, they were scared silly.

Nehemiah knew it, too. "And it happened when all our enemies heard of it, and all the nations around us saw these things, that they were very disheartened in their own eyes; for they perceived that this work was done by our God" (6:16).

"Very disheartened in their own eyes" means they were completely deflated—humiliated. These pompous, boasting agitators' worst dreams had come to pass, and before their eyes the city walls of Jerusalem had been resurrected out of the mounds of garbage. It was a glorious day for the people of God, and a nightmare come true for the likes of Sanballat and Tobiah.

What a contrast there is between those two and Nehemiah! Just six months earlier, they were gloating, strutting, self-serving potentates, and Nehemiah had been a servant in another ruler's palace. Now he was clearly in control of Jerusalem, and they were no more than common hoodlums, unwelcome and unable to get into the city they had once ruthlessly oppressed.

It's a study in cowardice and courage. Who could have predicted it would be this way? Just a few months before, Nehemiah had stood with his knees knocking in front of the king of Persia, sheepishly seeking permission to go to Jerusalem. "Then I became dreadfully afraid," he wrote of that moment in Nehemiah 2:2.

Could this be the same man who now listened to a prophet describe a treacherous plot against his life and confidently replied, "Should such a man as I flee? And who is there such as I who would go into the temple to save his life? I will not go in!" (6:11).

Such is the mark of a true champion. His only fear is that of falling short of the mark God has set for him. Compare the words of the apostle Paul, who wrote that the only thing he feared was "lest, when I have preached to others, I myself should become disqualified" (1 Cor. 9:27). It is significant that in all the New Testament epistles, believers are exhorted to fear only one thing: "Since a promise remains of entering His rest, let us fear lest any of you seem to have come short of it" (Heb. 4:1).

Any other kind of fear is out of place in the life and character of a champion, and Nehemiah was in every sense a true champion who did not fall short of the mark. Fearless and unmoving, he withstood every dart that Satan could hurl at him, and he emerged victorious as the builder of a great wall for God.

What are the secrets of his inner strength and courage? They are not difficult to observe in reading through his account.

God Will Fight for Us

Nehemiah gives one valuable insight after another into the problem of dealing with fear. First, see how he responded when rumors began to circulate that Sanballat and Tobiah were mounting a surprise attack. You can sense the fear of the builders (4:11–12):

> And our adversaries said, "They will neither know nor see anything, till we come into their midst and kill them and cause the work to cease." So it was, when the Jews who dwelt near them came, that they told us ten times, "From whatever place you turn, they will be upon us."

It was a frightening thought. Workmen were laboring on the wall around the full circumference of the city. Their backs were to the outside. They were vulnerable to attacks from any direction. And if attackers came from more than one side, they could be upon the workmen before they had time to group together for defense.

The subsequent verses describe how Nehemiah fortified the wall and set watchmen all around to signal any attack. I want to bypass that for the moment and call your attention to his reply to those who were fearful. We read in verses 19–20: "The work is great and extensive, and we are separated far from one another on the wall. Therefore, wherever you hear the sound of the trumpet, rally to us there. *Our God will fight for us*" (emphasis added).

Nehemiah knew the lessons from Old Testament history. He knew the stories of Moses, of Gideon, of David against Goliath. He knew the truth that "the battle is the LORD's" (1 Sam. 17:47). It is God who wins the real victories, and He never fails to fight for His people.

I wish people in our churches could learn that. There's so much being done today in the name of the Lord but in the power of the flesh. All of it is wasted effort. God has not abandoned His people! He still fights the battles for us if we'll let Him.

Let me tell you a secret: a battle fought in the power of the flesh is a battle lost, no matter what the apparent outcome. If it's worth winning, it's worth letting the Lord fight it for us. We don't win by might or by power, but by the Spirit of the Lord! (cf. Zech. 4:6). I get so weary of Christians who think they can organize and manipulate and campaign to elect this candidate or that, or pass this law or that, and change the world by voting out evil. Listen, if righteousness can be brought by law, then Christ died in vain (see Gal. 2:21).

When will we learn that the battle is the Lord's? The battle for men's souls is a spiritual battle, and it must be fought with spiritual weapons. We're not fighting against flesh and blood, "but against principalities, against powers, against the rulers of the darkness of this age, against spiritual hosts of wickedness in the heavenly places" (Eph. 6:12). That battle cannot be won through fleshly means.

Nehemiah succeeded because he let the Lord fight his battles. That's a pretty simple way to overcome the kind of stiff opposition he was up against, isn't it? Well, it *is* simple, but it's not simplistic. It's hard to let go and realize that "'vengeance is Mine, I will repay,' says the Lord" (Rom. 12:19).

When the Sanballats and Tobiahs come up against us with their jeering and threats, it's difficult to keep our silence and just look to the Lord to fight the battle. But that's what Nehemiah did.

We Will Fight, Too, if Necessary

Still, there is a sense in which we must be prepared to take up the sword, too. We can't fight the battle in the flesh, but just the same, we don't sit around while God does it alone.

Now, at first sight, you may feel there's a contradiction here, but not so. It's true that Nehemiah let the Lord fight the battle. It's just as true that he was prepared to take up arms and fight alongside the Lord.

The point is, he didn't jump into the battle in the power of the flesh. He armed himself so that if necessary, he could join the battle. Nehemiah never actually had to use his weapon in the battle. But he had his armor on, ready to fight if the Lord so directed.

Nehemiah 4:13-14 describes the measures he took:

> Therefore I positioned men behind the lower parts of
> the wall, at the openings, and I set the people ac-
> cording to their families, with their swords, their
> spears, and their bows. And I looked, and arose and
> said to the nobles, to the leaders, and to the rest of
> the people, "Do not be afraid of them. Remember
> the Lord, great and awesome, and fight for your
> brethren, your sons, your daughters, your wives,
> and your houses."

If God had called on Nehemiah to fight, he would have
gladly stepped in, I'm sure. But if that had been the case,
it would not have robbed God of complete credit for the
victory, any more than David's victory over Goliath could
be said to be the result of David's keen eye and great
strength. Clearly, it was the Lord alone who gave the victory.

Note Nehemiah's advice to the armed people on the
wall: "Do not be afraid of them. Remember the Lord,
great and awesome, and fight for your brethren, your
sons, your daughters, your wives, and your houses"
(v. 14).

"Remember the Lord, . . . and fight." A good balance.
It's the Lord who gives us the victory, and with that knowledge, we have the courage to fight.

The Israelites had always struggled with this concept.
There were times when they jumped into the fray in the
power of the flesh, thinking that their sheer numbers and
military acumen would win the day. And in those cases,
God always saw to it that they received a sound drubbing
at the hands of their enemies. First Samuel 4:2 tells of one

such battle: "Israel was defeated by the Philistines, who killed about four thousand men of the army in the field." It was a high price to pay for their fleshly cockiness.

There were other times when the Israelites thought God would fight for them and they could idly watch, and they were beaten just as soundly, or even more so. After that defeat at the hands of the Philistines, 1 Samuel 4:3-11 describes how the Israelites thought that if they just put the Ark of the Covenant at the front of their ranks, God would surely thrash their enemies with no effort on their part.

It didn't-happen. Verse 10 says, "So the Philistines fought, and Israel was defeated, and every man fled to his tent. There was a very great slaughter, and there fell of Israel thirty thousand foot soldiers."

In the first battle, their sin was pride. This time their sin was *presumption*. It was what Jesus spoke of when He quoted Deuteronomy 6:16 to the devil: "It is written again, 'You shall not tempt the LORD your God'" (Matt. 4:7). You don't just sit around and expect God to come to your aid like a genie in a lamp. You have to do your part as well. You have to put some feet to your prayers.

Moses grappled with this concept. I always smile at the account of Israel's escape from Pharaoh through the Red Sea. They almost didn't make it, because Moses stopped for a prayer meeting on the banks of the sea.

Pharaoh's armies had pursued the people of Israel until they could go no farther; before them lay an impassable body of water, and they had no boats. Moses was so sure of the Lord's deliverance, however, that he gathered the Israelites around him and gave this pep talk: "Do not be afraid. Stand still, and see the salvation of the LORD, which He will accomplish for you today. For the Egyptians whom you see today, you shall see again no more forever. The LORD will fight for you, and you shall hold your peace" (Exod. 14:13–14).

I like his faith, but that was not the time to be standing around. It was true that the Lord was going to fight for them, and it was true that the Egyptians would be destroyed to be seen no more. But God wasn't going to do it for a bunch of idle spectators. They had to get moving!

"And the LORD said to Moses, 'Why do you cry to Me?'" (There are times when prayer is *not* appropriate.) "'Tell the children of Israel to go forward'" (v. 15).

Moses was only half right when he said, "The LORD will fight for you, and you shall hold your peace." Better to have said, "The Lord will fight for you, and you shall do your part by running like crazy!" We can't hold our peace in times of conflict. We dare not usurp the Lord in the midst of the battle, but we can't afford to sit on the sidelines, either. Real courage comes in understanding the difference.

We Will Keep Building
While the Battle Rages

There's yet another aspect to Nehemiah's great courage, and it's the single most important element in his reaction to Sanballat's challenge. This is what brought ultimate victory in the short span of fifty-two days: Nehemiah did not turn away from his calling in order to fight the battle.

That's such a simple principle, but it is often forgotten completely. We're always in a battle with the forces of evil, but that's peripheral to our calling. We dare not let Satan's attacks turn us away from whatever it is that God has called us to do.

Herein is where Nehemiah's courage shines. He gave the battle to the Lord, yet he was prepared to fight. But even while fighting, he would be working on the wall. Read the account in Nehemiah 4:16–18:

> So it was, from that time on, that half of my servants worked at construction, while the other half held the spears, the shields, the bows, and wore armor; and the leaders were behind all the house of Judah. Those who built on the wall, and those who carried burdens, loaded themselves so that with one hand they worked at construction, and with the other held a weapon. Every one of the builders had his sword girded at his side as he built. And the one who sounded the trumpet was beside me.

Those soldier-builders must have been a sight! A trowel in one hand, a weapon in the other. If Sanballat and Tobiah had seen that, they surely would have quaked with terror at the determination of these militant stone masons.

This was not the garden variety courage. These people were serious! And a bully like Sanballat doesn't take on men of such courage. He never did go through with the threatened attack.

Read the rest of the account, from verses 21–23:

So we labored in the work, and half of the men held the spears from daybreak until the stars appeared. At the same time I also said to the people, "Let each man and his servant stay at night in Jerusalem, that they may be our guard by night and a working party by day." So neither I, my brethren, my servants, nor the men of the guard who followed me took off our clothes, except that everyone took them off for washing.

There was no stopping this man. He was prepared to fight, but not to abandon the work on the wall. This was a true champion, and we could all learn from his courage.

I suppose in the course of my ministry, I counsel more than a hundred people every month. I know from experience that every child of God is under satanic attack. Ephesians 6:11–18 tells us that; it should come as no surprise.

But I've noticed a clear pattern in those who seek spiritual advice: people who are willing to stick to their task, to be faithful to what God has called them to do—they are the ones who experience victory.

On the other hand, those who tremble and hide at the first sign of the devil's attack—they are the ones who fail, because they turn aside from whatever it is that God is calling them to do and focus all their attention on the enemy. And that is never a good idea.

The battle *is* the Lord's. He will give the victory. You can count on it. But be prepared to fight just the same. And above all, keep on working!

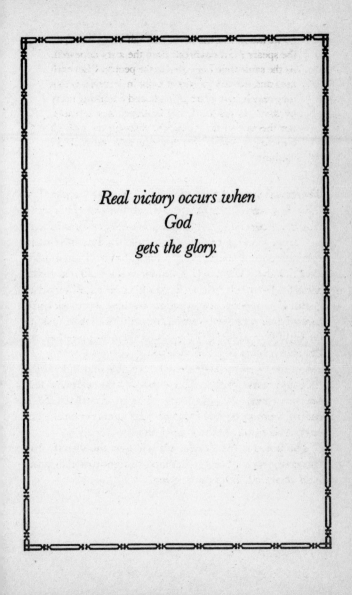

Real victory occurs when
God
gets the glory.

10

Sealing the Victory

With the city walls completed at last, a new spirit of civic and national identity was welling up in Jerusalem, and Nehemiah wanted to make the most of it.

First things first, and this was a priority that superseded even the dedication of the walls. The walls themselves were meaningless unless the formerly fragmented city inhabitants could be pulled together and unified.

Nehemiah had a plan for this, too, and we begin to see what it was in Nehemiah 7. What we observe here is a city moving from anarchy and confusion to a structured, more orderly way of life. Nehemiah wanted to consolidate the people. He would set the city in order, with new rulers, a new appreciation of their heritage, a new understanding of their family relationships, and above all a new dedication to their God. If Nehemiah could accomplish the reunification of the city, his victory would be complete.

A Feeling of Civic Progress

First, Nehemiah wanted to instill a good feeling about the progress of the city. The people had built the wall, and Jerusalem's former glory—or a significant measure of it—had been restored.

Note, however, that Nehemiah in no way took credit for the work that had been done, nor did he allow the people to gloat as if this had been their achievement. What they accomplished stands as one of the great successes of all time, but Nehemiah refused to allow the thrill of victory to make a difference in his character or attitude. He knew that ultimate victory comes when God gets the glory, and he was not one to accept adulation for what he had done as unto the Lord.

"This work was done by our God," Nehemiah declared (6:16). And it was true. Nehemiah had been the instrument, and God had used his hands; but it was God who conceived the project, laid it on Nehemiah's heart, supplied a workable plan by which to achieve it, granted the strength to endure, brought victory over opposition, and ultimately enabled the people to raise the wall. It was in every sense a work of God.

The people of Jerusalem were rejuvenated by the completion of the wall. It stirred them as they had not been stirred since the Temple was finished. They were a city again, and they could hold their heads high once more.

But the city needed leadership: "Then it was, when the wall was built and I had hung the doors, when the gatekeepers, the singers, and the Levites had been appointed, that I gave the charge of Jerusalem to my brother Hanani, and Hananiah the leader of the citadel, for he was a faithful man and feared God more than many" (7:1–2).

Nehemiah was the governor of the city, the *Tirshatha* appointed by the king, to represent the empire officially. As such, he had the authority to appoint deputies. Being the great leader that he was, Nehemiah knew the wisdom of delegation.

He appointed two men, his brother Hanani and Hananiah, to become governors of the city. You remember Hanani. He was one of those back in Nehemiah 1:2 who first reported to Nehemiah the need to rebuild the walls. He didn't stay in Persia and let Nehemiah do all the work; he had returned with his brother. As Nehemiah's brother, he was a good choice for deputy. Who better to represent the champion in leadership than his close brother? The other deputy was Hananiah. Similar names, but they were different men. It is important to note Nehemiah's reason for choosing Hananiah: because he was a godly, faithful man.

That is always point number one in God's criteria for leadership. Throughout the New Testament pastoral epistles, whenever God cites the qualifications for church leadership, the key to everything is that God's leaders have to be men who are blameless and above reproach, godly in every sense (cf. 1 Tim. 3; Titus 1:6–9). It's not necessarily the most successful businessmen who make the best leaders in the economy of God. It is faithful, godly, diligent men, because they alone are equipped to lead by example.

Apparently that's what Nehemiah wanted—men like himself, who could lead the people by example. Let me point out here again that Nehemiah was not grabbing the glory for himself. He could have said, "OK, *I* led you in building the wall. It was *my* idea, and *I* organized and carried it off. And *I* think *I* should be your new ruler." No. He delegated that task to other qualified individuals.

There's a huge risk in turning authority over to another person; that person may fail, and the work you've labored so hard to build might be destroyed. Every preacher who has ever left one church to go on to another struggles with this fear. But inevitably in any growing work, the time comes when authority must be delegated. It's best to accept this as a necessity of life and carefully select qualified individuals to designate as the new leaders. That's what Nehemiah did.

Now that the walls were up and the gates were functioning, Nehemiah wanted to get full use of them. He gave this unusual order in Nehemiah 7:3: "And I said to them, 'Do not let the gates of Jerusalem be opened until the sun is hot; and while they stand guard, let them shut the doors and bar them; and appoint guards from among the inhabitants of Jerusalem, one at his watch station and another in front of his own house.'"

It was normal for the gates to be opened at daybreak, but Nehemiah wanted the people to be more watchful than that. They were to leave the gates closed until late in the morning. In addition, guards would be posted at the sealed gates around the clock.

Was there some great danger? No more now than before. But because the walls were new, now was a critical time to fortify them against attack, lest some enemy decide early to test their effectiveness. Nehemiah knew, also, that walls are not an infallible defense. After all, Babylon had fallen to Persia because the city walls weren't carefully guarded, and the enemy had crept over the side in the night. Nehemiah, as a servant in the Persian royal palace, knew the story well.

But more than all that, I believe this was part of Nehemiah's strategy to consolidate the people. He wanted to instill in them a strong sense of civic progress and a feeling of community. Before the walls were built, they had hidden alone in their houses at night for fear of marauders. Now they would work in teams to guard their new gates.

A Feeling of National Pride

Nehemiah also realized that walls alone don't make a great city. The walls were a magnificent accomplishment, but not a cure-all. Now he had to bring the people of the city together with a new sense of national identity. And to do that, it was necessary that they go back to their roots. That led to a very practical kind of history lesson.

Nehemiah had dug around in some old scrolls and located a genealogical record. It was just the thing for the time, because it would be the key to bringing a sense of history and destiny to a people that had for years been living in indifference to their great heritage.

The Jewish nation was unique. Chosen by God to be the bloodline through which He would bring the Messiah into the world, they had a special interest in genealogies. Read the great genealogies that trace the lineage of Jesus Christ back through Abraham to Adam (see Matt. 1:1–17; Luke 3:23–38).

It was important that these records be maintained. A

Jewish person's heritage was more important to him than his social status in many ways. If he was a Levite, for example, his life's work was already established. Every Jewish child knew which tribe he came from, and many of them could recite genealogies that went back for centuries.

Nehemiah wrote, "Then my God put it into my heart to gather the nobles, the rulers, and the people, that they might be registered by genealogy. And I found a register of the genealogy of those who had come up in the first return" (7:5).

It was God who put this plan into his heart, and Nehemiah recognized that. As he read the genealogy, notice that he singled out three significant groups of people.

He first mentioned them in verse 1: "the gatekeepers, the singers, and the Levites." He mentioned them again in verses 43–45:

> *The Levites:* the children of Jeshua, of Kadmiel, and of the children of Hodevah, seventy-four. *The singers:* the children of Asaph, one hundred and forty-eight. *The gatekeepers:* the children of Shallum, the children of Ater, the children of Talmon, the children of Akkub, the children of Hatita, the children of Shobai, one hundred and thirty-eight. (emphasis added)

And once more Nehemiah referred to them in the final verse of chapter 7: "So the priests, the Levites, the gatekeepers, the singers, some of the people, the Nethinim, and all Israel dwelt in their cities" (v. 73).

Who were these three groups of people? The Levites you surely know already. They were the tribe from which the priests and workers in the Temple came. As a tribe they had no land, but they lived on the tithes given by the Israelites. Their chief job was offering sacrifices.

The singers? Well, you can figure out what they did, but it may surprise you to learn that there was an officially designated group of them. Yes, Nehemiah had a choir. These were people gifted in music, whose job it was to offer praises in song. I doubt that singing was their full-time occupation, but much like the church choirs of today, they made up the sanctuary chorus and led the people in singing praise. That this was viewed as an important role is evident in the fact that they were one of only three groups singled out by Nehemiah.

The role of the gatekeepers was also fairly obvious. They hadn't had much work to do in Jerusalem for several years, but now business was hopping! They had through Nehemiah been elevated to one of the most visible and appreciated roles in the reconstructed city. While the priests took care of the sacrifices and the singers took care of the songs, they would oversee the security of Jerusalem.

The three groups lent to the nation an invigorated sense of unity and mission. Each had a unique task to do, and together they served the chosen nation of the living God. They were an important part of the new nationalism of Israel.

A genealogy is not very exciting unless it's your own, but Nehemiah's reading of the genealogy captivated the people's attention. They were gaining a new sense of national pride, and they all wanted to know that their place in the nation was secure.

Unhappily, that was not the case for some. Verses 61–

65 tell of a group who had to be put out of the priesthood because their lineage was polluted. Someone in their line had married into heathenism.

At first glance, this may appear to be grossly unfair. These men had lived in the city and worked as priests, perhaps for years. It is likely that they worked alongside the others on the wall. Now, suddenly, because their names could not be found in the genealogical records, should they be unceremoniously put out of the priesthood and disfellowshiped from the nation?

It was difficult, but it had to be done. God's law had to be obeyed without compromise. These men could never qualify as priests, but if they were genuine in their faith, and if they wanted to follow Jewish law, they could join Israel as proselytes (cf. Exod. 12:48–49). They were not excluded from worship or fellowship, but they were excluded from serving in the priesthood. That's the way it had to be if purity was to be maintained.

After all, this was a central lesson in the building of the wall: the wall was there to keep the people of God in and the corrupting influences of the Gentile nations out. Israel had fought and frequently lost that battle throughout her history.

The genealogy was read, a census was taken, and once again after decades of captivity, the Jewish nation was taking form—but it was only a remnant. Of the millions of Jews that left the land in the captivity, only 42,360 had returned (see 7:66).

A Feeling of Family Purpose

There was much work yet to be done. In 7:4, Nehemiah noted, "Now the city was large and spacious, but the people in it were few, and the houses were not rebuilt."

Forty-two thousand people, and Nehemiah wrote, "The people in it were few"? That's right. Most of those people lived outside the city, in small huts and makeshift villages nearby.

In the reading of the genealogies, Nehemiah accomplished one more important goal: he gave each family a sense of purpose. They were never meant to be independent groups of people huddled in tiny tent cities. They weren't vagabonds. They were all part of one great nation, chosen by God, whose families all had rich heritages. They were the children of Abraham.

Now that the city was rebuilt, Nehemiah wanted to bring people within its walls. The city was not large enough to house everyone, but those who wanted to could move into Jerusalem.

Nehemiah 11:1–2 describes the process that was followed: "Now the leaders of the people dwelt at Jerusalem; the rest of the people cast lots to bring one out of ten to dwell in Jerusalem, the holy city, and nine-tenths were to dwell in other cities. And the people blessed all the men who willingly offered themselves to dwell at Jerusalem." One in ten could come to Jerusalem; the rest were free to dwell in other cities.

I like Nehemiah's emphasis on the family. Even when the walls were under construction, Nehemiah had families working together. Nehemiah 3 is the list of all who worked on the walls. Notice that they were listed according to families. And pay attention to something else worthy of note: Nehemiah had everyone working as close to home as possible:

> Next to them Jedaiah the son of Harumaph made repairs *in front of his house.* . . . .After him Benjamin and Hasshub made repairs *opposite their house.* After them Azariah the son of Maaseiah, the son of Ananiah, made repairs *by his house.* . . . Beyond the Horse Gate the priests made repairs *each in front of his own house.* After them Zadok the son of Immer made repairs *in front of his own house.* After him Shemaiah the son of Shechaniah, the keeper of the East Gate made repairs. After him Hananiah the son of Shelemiah, and Hanun, the sixth son of Zalaph, repaired another section. After him Meshullam the son of Berechiah made repairs *in front of his dwelling.* (3:10, 23, 28–30, emphasis added)

Nehemiah wanted these men to work near their homes and families. It wouldn't do to have men working day and night on the wall, believing they were doing a work for God, yet out of touch with their families.

That happens too often in Christian work—and in secular work, for that matter. Listen, you can't serve God and neglect your family! What good is it if you spend your life preaching to unbelievers in the world but you aren't investing the time necessary to bring your own children up in the nurture and admonition of the Lord?

Nehemiah clung to a truth that the twentieth-century

world has discarded: a nation is only as strong as its families. No nation can survive long if the basic building block of society, the family, is destroyed.

Our world today is saturated with homeless people, parentless children, single parents, uncared-for elderly people, and people otherwise unattached to solid, caring families. We're moving more and more toward a society where the individual, not the family, is most significant. That has given way to a great sense of fear and aloneness, because when you remove the family, you remove the individual's basic support.

The decline of the family is killing our society. Unmarried couples living together have long since ceased to be stigmatized. Homosexual marriages are now widely accepted as legitimate alternatives to the traditional family. Working mothers deposit their children in day care centers and leave them for someone else to raise. It's a national tragedy! More than half the couples that get married this year will be divorced before their tenth anniversary. And even Christian families are not immune to the problems that plague the rest of society. We are losing the same ground Nehemiah was working so hard to gain.

Definite, observable progress had been made in Jerusalem. The city was coming back to life with vigor. But one important matter—unquestionably the most important item of all—had to be resolved. If the victory was to be really complete, Nehemiah had to turn the people back to the Word of God.

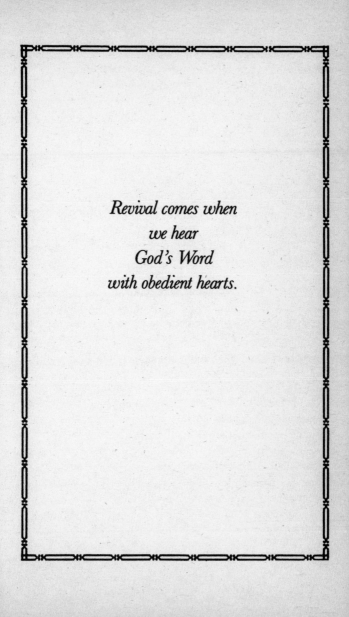

Revival comes when
we hear
God's Word
with obedient hearts.

11

The Other *Water Gate*

The book of Nehemiah is filled with good things. The characters are wonderful; you have the wise leader and man of action versus the corrupt and diabolical Sanballat and Tobiah. The plot is a treasure; against all odds, the people of God pull off an incredible feat by building the wall in fifty-two days. And on top of that, it is filled with lessons for modern-day people about leadership, about lay service, about how to deal with personal attacks, and about making the most of divine opportunity.

I love the entire book, but I have to admit that my favorite part of all is chapters 8–10. There we have the record of one of the most marvelous revivals God ever sent. I can't read it without my own heart's being stirred by a longing to see revival in our time.

Nothing is more stimulating to me than to see revival at

work in the hearts of men and women. Stay with me; we're going to see the people of God storm the gates of hell and reclaim precious ground they had yielded to Satan years before.

This is a far more significant event, much more of a miracle, than the building of a wall. It's one thing for the people of God to dig through the trash heap for rocks to put one on top of another. It is quite a different spectacle to see God take those people and make them living stones, "built up a spiritual house, a holy priesthood, to offer up spiritual sacrifices acceptable to God" (1 Pet. 2:5).

God was doing some stone masonry of His own, in a spiritual sense, on His people. He was going to take away their hearts of stone and give them new hearts.

The Reading of the Law

Nehemiah 8:1-4 sets the scene for the start of the revival:

> Now all the people gathered together as one man in the open square that was in front of the Water Gate; and they told Ezra the scribe to bring the Book of the Law of Moses, which the LORD had commanded Israel. So Ezra the priest brought the Law before the congregation, of men and women and all who could hear with understanding, on the first day of the seventh month. Then he read from it in the open square that was in front of the Water Gate from morning until midday, before the men and women and those who could understand; and the ears of all the people were attentive to the Book of the Law. So

> Ezra the scribe stood on a platform of wood which
> they had made for the purpose.

Isn't that a sight? There were more people there than at a twentieth-century college football game, patiently standing in the street, listening as Ezra read from God's Word. There were no public address systems in those days, of course, so everyone had to be very still.

They had gathered by the water gate, the place where fresh water could be brought in. It was an important place, central to the life support of the community. They didn't know it, but they were about to receive rivers of living water, supplying them with a kind of life the nation had forgotten was possible.

This is the first glimpse we have had of Ezra in the book of Nehemiah. Most Bible students believe he had been away from Jerusalem for several years and returned especially for this great event. At any rate, there he was, God's faithful priest, reading the Word of God at the top of his lungs.

Ezra and Nehemiah make an interesting contrast. Ezra was the archetypical scholar—a godly, studious man who had given his life to understanding and teaching the Word of God. Nehemiah, on the other hand, was the man of action—the zealous, aggressive reformer. God had used them both in mighty ways.

That's the way it is with the servants of God. Not all of them are alike. God has His scholars, and He has His doers. They all are given unique ministries according to how they're gifted. God is not trying to crank out assembly-line evangelists all patterned after one model.

He makes and gifts each one of us separately. No matter who you are or how God has gifted you, He has a special ministry designed for you. Find out what it is, and do it with all your heart.

Both Ezra and Nehemiah *had* served God with all their hearts, and as different as they were, I know they both rejoiced to see this day. The people of God were assembled to hear His Word.

God's Word is the essential element in every revival. There has never been a spiritual revival in all of human history that did not have its roots in the Word of God. Why? Because that's where the real power is. Apart from God's Word, there is no basis for revival. It is Scripture alone that is "living, and powerful, and sharper than any two-edged sword, piercing even to the division of soul and spirit, and of joints and marrow, and is a discerner of the thoughts and intents of the heart" (Heb. 4:12).

When these people heard God's Word firsthand—many of them, I'm convinced, for the first time—their hearts were stirred. The two-edged sword was probing, doing precision surgery on the cold and stony hearts of the hearers.

This was one of the largest worship services assembled in a long time. And they were serious about worshiping. Verses 5–8 of chapter 8 give the order of service:

> And Ezra opened the book in the sight of all the people, for he was standing above all the people; and when he opened it, all the people stood up. And Ezra blessed the LORD, the great God. Then all the people answered, "Amen, Amen!" while lifting up

their hands. And they bowed their heads and worshiped the LORD with their faces to the ground. Also Jeshua, Bani, Sherebiah, Jamin, Akkub, Shabbethai, Hodijah, Maaseiah, Kelita, Azariah, Jozabad, Hanan, Pelaiah, and the Levites, *helped the people to understand* the Law; and the people stood in their place. So they read distinctly from the book, in the Law of God; *and they gave the sense, and helped them to understand* the reading. (emphasis added)

Did you catch that phrase "and they gave the sense, and helped them to understand"? To me, this is the most significant statement in the whole record of the revival. It is a biblical description of what the preaching of God's Word should be. You can have your pretty homiletics; just give me the sense of God's Word. *That's* biblical preaching.

I'm concerned about the move away from biblical preaching in our churches today. We emphasize entertainment. We feature Christian celebrities. We listen to testimonies. We do drama. We keep everybody happy, but preaching is getting the short end of the stick.

We can't get away from this as the central feature of genuine worship: the Word of God must be proclaimed, and the sense of it must be given. That's the only thing that can bring revival, and that's the only thing that can change people's lives.

Look at the immediate response of the people to God's Word. They repented. In fact, they were so devastated by a sense of their own sin that Ezra had to remind them that this was to be a time of rejoicing!

And Nehemiah, who was the governor, Ezra the priest and scribe, and the Levites who taught the people said to all the people, "This day is holy to the LORD your God; do not mourn nor weep." For all the people wept, when they heard the words of the Law. Then he said to them, "Go your way, eat the fat, drink the sweet, and send portions to those for whom nothing is prepared; for this day is holy to our LORD. Do not sorrow, for the joy of the LORD is your strength." So the Levites quieted all the people, saying, "Be still, for the day is holy; do not be grieved." (8:9–12)

Repentance and rejoicing are not incompatible, by the way. True repentance often accompanies a deep sorrow for sins, but it never fails to make the heart glad, because the burden of sin is instantly lifted.

The inhabitants of Jerusalem were about to learn that God's mercy and grace are infinitely greater than all their sin, compounded as it had been over the centuries.

Remember, these were God's people, repenting from their sin. That's where revival always starts—in the household of God. Unbelievers can't be revived; they've never been "vived" in the first place. You can't restore life to something that has always been lifeless. Unbelievers can be saved, and that's usually a side effect of true revival, but it is not what constitutes revival.

By the way, you might notice that Sanballat's name is strangely missing from the second half of the book of Nehemiah. He's mentioned only once, in 13:28, about four verses before Nehemiah closed his memoirs. And I find this more than a little amusing: "And one of the sons of Joiada, the son of Eliashib the high priest, was a son-in-law of Sanballat the Horonite; therefore I drove him from me."

Whatever happened to old Sanballat? He was gone from the scene. In the beginning of the book, he kept showing up, like a pesky fly that buzzes around your face. But now he was gone, and all that was left was for Nehemiah to chase his son-in-law out of town.

You see, Satan's gadflies don't last long in the face of real spiritual power. Sanballat thought he had trouble with Nehemiah. What was he going to do now that the whole city had been revived? He could either get saved or get out, and it looks as though he chose the latter.

The revival was just beginning. The initial reading of God's Word, scheduled to last a day, would turn into a full-scale, month-long Bible conference. The people's appetites had been whetted, and they wanted more.

The Observance of the Feast

Day two of the revival was to revolutionize the nation:

> Now on the second day the heads of the fathers' houses of all the people, with the priests and Levites, were gathered to Ezra the scribe, in order to understand the words of the Law. And they found written in the Law, which the LORD had commanded by Moses, that the children of Israel should dwell in booths during the feast of the seventh month, and that they should announce and proclaim in all their

> cities and in Jerusalem, saying, "Go out to the
> mountain, and bring olive branches, branches of oil
> trees, myrtle branches, palm branches, and
> branches of leafy trees, to make booths, as it is writ-
> ten." (8:13–15)

As they were reading through Scripture, the people found truth that had long gone unobeyed. It was the time of the Feast of Tabernacles. Israel had not observed that feast for generations. Now they wanted to do it with enthusiasm.

This was wholehearted obedience. They threw themselves into it with great vigor. Verse 17 tells us that this feast had not been observed with that kind of eagerness since the days of Joshua.

It wasn't convenient to observe the Feast of Tabernacles. Each family had to build little booths to dwell in for seven days. It was a little like pitching a pup tent and moving the family in for a week. Not a fun thing to do, especially if you had children. But it was a memorial to bring to remembrance all that God had done for the Israelites in the wilderness during Moses' time, and it was a feast with rich spiritual meaning to people just coming out of the wilderness of sin and captivity.

Inconvenience was not an issue with these people anyway. They were so excited to be back in fellowship with God that if they had to live in booths for a week, they would do it with gusto. Meanwhile, their insatiable thirst for the Word of God grew.

Verse 18 says, "Also day by day, from the first day until the last day, he read from the book of the Law of God." There was nothing in the instructions for the Feast of Tabernacles that required the people to listen to the public reading of Scripture for that week. But they so wanted to hear the Bible that they kept it up every day.

That hunger for God's Word is one of the sure signs of genuine revival. When God stirs your heart, He always plants in it a longing for His truth.

The Sealing of the Covenant

Now the revival hit with full force. The feast had ended, and the restrained sense of sorrow the people had felt because of their sin swept over them like a tidal wave. These people meant business: "Now on the twenty-fourth day of this month the children of Israel were assembled with fasting, in sackcloth, and with dust on their heads. Then those of Israelite lineage separated themselves from all foreigners; and they stood and confessed their sins and the iniquities of their fathers" (9:1-2).

Look how they spent the day: "And they stood up in their place and read from the Book of the Law of the LORD their God for one-fourth of the day; and for another fourth they confessed and worshiped the LORD their God" (v. 3). What a precious time they had before the Lord!

The prayer that follows in Nehemiah 9 is one of the longest prayers recorded anywhere in all of Scripture. In it, the Levites led the people in a prayer of repentance in which they recited the goodness of God to them throughout their history.

The scene closes as the people sealed their repentance with a special vow. It was a covenant they made together before God, admitting their failure to obey His Word and committing themselves to serve Him faithfully.

Chapter 10 of Nehemiah records their covenant. By God's design, that covenant became a part of His eternal, infallible Word. It is worthwhile noting the seven elements of the covenant: that they would not marry the heathen (see 10:30); that they would observe the Sabbath (see v. 31); that they would observe the Sabbath year (see v. 31); that they would pay the Temple tax (see vv. 32-33); that they would keep the altar burning (see v. 34); that they would tithe what was rightfully the Lord's (see vv. 35-38); and that they would not forsake God's house (see v. 39).

It was a huge step forward for the people of God—like nothing since the days of David. Nehemiah's victory was at last complete.

The Renewal of the Nation

"Watergate" to Americans evokes images of scandal and shame. This water gate, however, was something completely different. It was the rebirth of God's chosen nation. This is the last great revival recorded for us in Old Testament times. From this point to the time of Christ, there were four centuries of silence.

But this revival was tremendously important. It revitalized the nation of Israel. It gave the people a renewed interest in and appreciation for the Word of God. Who knows? Without the work of Nehemiah and the effects of this revival, the Word of God and the Israelite nation could well have been lost forever.

Out of this revival came an interest in Scripture that was unprecedented and has never been equaled. A new movement of scribes rose up, dedicated to preserving the Word of God and making it widely available, and they began feverishly to copy and disseminate the Word of God. Most of the Old Testament manuscripts from which we draw the Hebrew text today are the heritage of this movement.

It all began because the people heard God's Word with obedient hearts. Revival always begins when men and women break down and weep over their sins and begin to make right their disobedience. May we be challenged to come to Scripture always with that kind of openness!

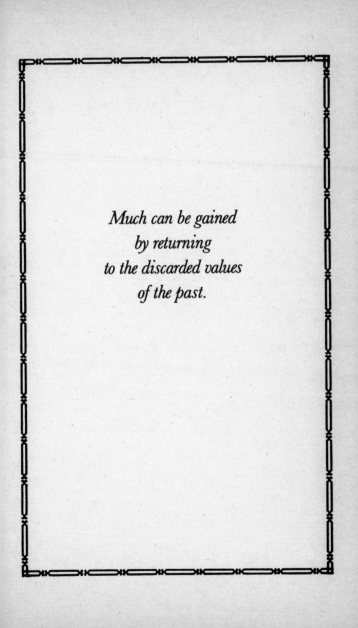

*Much can be gained
by returning
to the discarded values
of the past.*

12

New Walls from the Debris of the Old

*A*fter the great Chicago fire in 1872, there were many who believed the city itself would die. The conflagration that destroyed Chicago was unprecedented in modern history, and there was so much loss, so many families dispossessed, so many buildings destroyed, and so little left that most observers were certain it was the end of the city.

A newspaper reporter who happened to be on the scene, however, said he was amazed upon surveying the ruins to find that even before the flames were completely extinguished, undaunted Chicago residents were rebuilding a new city on top of the ashes of the old.

In fact, Grant Park, that beautiful green area on the lakefront of downtown Chicago, almost entirely consists of land that was reclaimed from Lake Michigan, built up by pushing the ruins of the burned city into the lake to make room for new buildings! When you walk through Grant Park in Chicago, you are walking on what is left of the ashes of the great Chicago fire.

Nehemiah went a step further than that: he rebuilt Jerusalem by *using* the ruins of the destroyed city. The new wall was constructed from the boulders of the old, and there it stands today, a constant reminder of the grace of God, who can pick up the pieces of ruined cities, nations, or lives and make of them something new and glorious.

Imagine what a testimony that wall was to the people of Jerusalem—in fact, to everyone who lived in the region. They had seen the piles of overgrown boulders and garbage that had surrounded the city for more than a century. They knew that God's judgment had fallen on the city and the entire nation. The broken walls had been a mute testimony for decades to the fact that God judges sin.

Now those same boulders stood one on top of another, making an entirely different kind of statement. Thus, the wall was a monument to the grace and forgiveness of Jehovah. God, whose wrath against His people's sin had permitted the walls to be torn down, was the only One whose power was sufficient to resurrect those walls so quickly.

One Final Detail

One last detail had to be seen to before the wall could be dedicated. The city needed to be repopulated, as we saw earlier. There were not enough people living in Jerusalem. The wall around the outside had been rebuilt, and it was now a viable city, but it lacked one very important item every city must have—a population. Houses could not be built easily before the city was secure, but now that the wall was up, let the internal construction begin!

The city was open to anyone who wanted to move in, but there weren't enough volunteers. No one likes to relocate, especially if it requires rebuilding. The plan to get enough people to move was this: draw lots. One in ten would be selected that way to move inside the walls.

In order for that plan to work, the people had to be willing. That's a major hurdle; it is a rare individual who will say, "I'll go where you want me to go, dear Lord," and mean it. But in the revived atmosphere around Jerusalem, Nehemiah had little difficulty convincing the people that they could trust God to lead them the right way. Several people offered to relocate outright, and everyone was willing to participate in the lot-drawing, as we read before from the beginning verses of Nehemiah 11.

The remainder of Nehemiah 11 and half of chapter 12 is the register of the people and where they lived. This is a marvelous document. It is the record of a people preserved by God through years of captivity, brought back to the land, restored, revived, revitalized, and relocated, ready to serve Jehovah whatever the cost—as His chosen people were meant to do.

Malachi 3:16 probably refers to this very document: "Those who feared the LORD spoke to one another, and the LORD listened and heard them; so a book of remembrance was written before Him for those who fear the LORD and who meditate on His name." This was a list of the faithful, those who thought about the Lord and talked about Him to one another.

Jerusalem was finally the kind of community God designed it to be, a place where "those who feared the LORD spoke to one another." It was a place where God could be glorified in the midst of His people. The walls were ready for dedication.

A Day to Remember

Dedication day represented the pinnacle of Nehemiah's life. Those walls were the tangible result of his life's work. The proof of God's hand on Nehemiah was all around, in the spirit of the people and the new sense of national destiny they shared. He had indeed been used of God to build something new and glorious out of the rubbish of the past.

The dedication of a structure was a normal part of the Hebrew culture (cf. Deut. 20:5). The dedication of any building was a spiritual act of consecration and inauguration. No construction project was truly complete until it had been dedicated.

A great ceremony was planned:

> Now at the dedication of the wall of Jerusalem they sought out the Levites in all their places, to bring them to Jerusalem to celebrate the dedication with gladness, both with thanksgivings and singing, with cymbals and stringed instruments and harps. And the sons of the singers gathered together. . . . Then the priests and Levites purified themselves, and purified the people, the gates, and the wall. (12:27–30)

Remember the gatekeepers, the singers, and the Levites? They were all in attendance, and it was a glorious day.

The people, the priests, and even the wall were ceremonially purified. Then Nehemiah divided the people into two great groups:

> So I brought the leaders of Judah up on the wall, and appointed two large thanksgiving choirs, one of which went to the right hand on the wall toward the Refuse Gate. . . . The other thanksgiving choir went the opposite way, and I was behind them with half of the people on the wall, going past the Tower of the Ovens as far as the Broad Wall . . . . and they stopped by the Gate of the Prison. So the two thanksgiving choirs stood in the house of God, likewise I and the half of the rulers with me. . . . Also that day they offered great sacrifices, and rejoiced, for God had made them rejoice with great joy; the women and the children also rejoiced, so that the joy of Jerusalem was heard afar off. (vv. 31–43)

Everyone got involved, and it was a time of great blessing and praise. The ceremony must have been a long one; it surely took a while for those two great groups of people to walk around the circumference of the wall. Ezra led one group, Nehemiah led the other, and they met on the other side.

A Foundation to Build On

That walk around the wall served as an object lesson to all who were there that day. They saw firsthand the work they had wrought in God's strength. They had all worked together on the wall; it was not the work of any single individual. Yet the completed wall was a unified structure, like the nation made of many tribes.

What they had learned in the building of the wall and the revival that followed is an important lesson to all of us: much is to be gained by returning to the discarded values of the past. There is no new and different truth to be learned that can revolutionize the world. What is needed is a treasure hunt through the garbage piles of wreckage left by previous generations and past disobediences. The principles and values that were thrown away through the sins of the past can be retrieved to be rebuilt into something that will honor God.

Nehemiah's wall was like a new foundation, a fresh start for Israel to build upon. The shattered people of God were back together in the land, and the wall stood as a reminder that God could redeem even the failures of the past. With God all things are possible—even a new wall from the rubble of the old.

Or a new life from the wreckage of old sin.

The revived and restored people of God were home at last. Nehemiah's great dream had been realized. He had led the people faithfully, miraculously, under the hand of God, to do the impossible. To God be the glory.

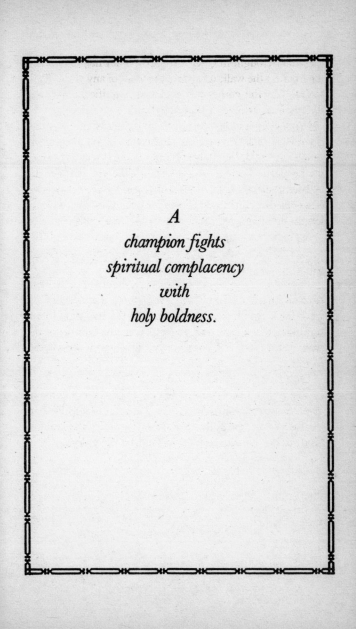

A
champion fights
spiritual complacency
with
holy boldness.

13

The Real Work Begins When the Job Is Finished

*N*ehmiah's story would have been prettier without the thirteenth chapter of his book. It adds a bit of sadness to his story that I wish were not there. But it is, and it makes the account more real.

One of the sad facts of revival is that it doesn't last forever. God's people grow complacent, and sin creeps into the routine, while the glory of revival fades away. It happened over and over in the Word of God, and Nehemiah's ministry in Jerusalem provides one more example.

In one sense, however, I'm glad to get this final glimpse of God's great champion as he stood up against the abuses of evil, called sin by name, and demanded that God's people obey the covenant they signed. It's exhilarating to see that he hadn't lost his vigor, his holy indignation against unrighteousness. He was patching some cracks in the wall.

Lest the Walls Come Tumbling Down

Nehemiah was jealous for God—in the good sense. He resented it when people who knew better sinned sins of presumption and outright disobedience. And he was concerned lest the creeping influence of sin in society eat away at the mortar that held it all together, and lest the walls he worked so hard to build begin to crumble again.

Nehemiah had been away from Jerusalem for a while. He didn't say how long, but we assume it was several years. That would explain his shock and anger (see 13:8) at the way sin had crept into his city.

You remember that when Nehemiah first sought the king's permission to go to Jerusalem, he promised the king that he would return after certain days. He had set a time when he planned to return (see 2:6). Perhaps that time had come, and Nehemiah had returned to Shushan to fill out his service to the king. Then he gained permission once again to return to Jerusalem: "In the thirty-second year of Artaxerxes king of Babylon I had returned to the king. Then after certain days I obtained leave from the king" (13:6).

Upon his return to Jerusalem, Nehemiah was confronted with several abuses. First, astonishingly, the high priest had let Nehemiah's old nemesis Tobiah move into a room in the Temple! Nehemiah was outraged. Man of action that he was, he moved quickly: "I threw all the household goods of Tobiah out of the room" (v. 8). Then he made the priests scrub down the room and cleanse it.

Good for you, Nehemiah! This was no time for diplomacy. The man wasn't even an Israelite. He was a foe of the nation and an enemy of God. He had no right living in the Temple. Nehemiah's action evokes a picture of the Lord Jesus, who, similarly outraged that the Temple should become a haven for evildoers, turned over tables and drove the money changers out.

This kind of holy boldness is often not well received by religious people, but it is always necessary when the enemy moves into the Temple. Once I was preaching in a tent meeting in Brisbane, Australia. The tent had been pitched right across the street from a tavern, and the devil didn't like the competition. Occasionally, drunks from the tavern would stumble into the tent meeting and disturb the services. One night a couple of drunkards came in and began to heckle me while I was preaching. They were particularly noisy and distracting, so I asked some of the volunteer ushers to escort them out.

"Why?" the ushers challenged me. "They aren't hurting you."

But they *were* disturbing the meeting and keeping people from hearing God's Word. There was only one thing left for me to do. I couldn't contain my righteous indignation. I literally took the hecklers by the nape of the neck and the seat of the pants and threw them out of the tent. And I ordered them to stay away until they were sober.

The church people in the crowd were shocked! In fact, I think most of them were more shocked at me than they had been at the men's drunkenness. But God honored my boldness; the next night more than four hundred people came to hear the crazy American evangelist. The drunkards never disturbed another meeting, and dozens of people came to Christ for the first time.

Remember the Covenant!

Nehemiah was also displeased to learn that the terms of the covenant signed by all the people in chapter 10 were being forgotten. For one thing, the tithes had not been kept up (see 13:10). The Levites and Temple musicians had not been paid.

"So I contended with the rulers, and said, 'Why is the house of God forsaken?' And I gathered them together and set them in their place" (v. 11). Someone needed to put them in their place. It's amazing how easily sincere people abandon a vow they have made before God in the apathy of a postrevival mentality.

"Contended" means "fought with," "argued with," "opposed vehemently." Nehemiah was angry, and he had a right to be. The people were moving away from the commitment of their vows.

There were other abuses. The Sabbath was being violated (see vv. 15–18). Nehemiah had a response to that. He ordered the gates closed on the Sabbath, and he locked the defilers outside for the day! I like his challenge to them in verse 21: "If you do so again, I will lay hands on you!" That was not a reference to the kind of laying on of hands we normally think of in the church!

His methods were crude, but very effective. "From that time on they came no more on the Sabbath" (v. 21).

Everything was at stake here. All the ground that had been gained during Nehemiah's first stay in Jerusalem was now in danger of being forfeited. Why? Because the people had grown careless and lazy.

Take note of this: it isn't usually outright rebellion that

causes godly people to backslide. It's carelessness, apathy, sloth, and dullness. We too easily forget the vow we swore in the height of revival. And when we abandon those sacred commitments, we slide directly into the mire of the darkest kinds of sin.

That's what was happening in Jerusalem, and Nehemiah was there to shake things up!

Cleansing the City Again

An insidious thing was beginning to happen, too. The city was being infiltrated by strangers. Men of Israel had begun to marry pagan women, and outsiders had moved into the city. What good was a wall around the city of God if the heathen were allowed to come and go as they wished?

Nehemiah was fighting mad—literally. His life's work was being threatened by the reckless compromise of careless men. "So I contended with them and cursed them, struck some of them and pulled out their hair, and made them swear by God, saying, 'You shall not give your daughters as wives to their sons, nor take their daughters for your sons or yourselves'" (v. 25).

A spiritual response? In this case, yes. Their sin was an outrage, and it called for an outrageous application of justice. Remember, this wasn't an act of personal retaliation, but the response of a man jealous for God's glory. The people had broken their solemn and sacred vow, and extreme measures were called for to remedy the situation.

In this final chapter of the story of Nehemiah's life, we see a side of him we have never before seen. In response to

Sanballat and Tobiah he had always just prayed, and God had defended him. Now we see him as a kicking, screaming, cursing, hair-pulling, wild-eyed brawler. What had happened to change him thus?

There's a good reason for his personality change. Something altogether different was at stake now than when Sanballat and Tobiah were waging their war against him. Then it was Nehemiah's work, his character, his reputation, his pride. He didn't count those things as worthy of defending. Now, however, it was God who was being attacked. His work, His character, His reputation, His glory were at stake. And those things *are* worth fighting for.

Sanballat and Tobiah had attacked Nehemiah, and God had defended him. Now the backsliding Israelites were attacking God's righteousness, and Nehemiah was ready to fight on the Lord's behalf.

This time in Nehemiah's life must have been the most difficult of all for him. He was nearing the end of his ministry, and he had waged many battles with the enemy. Now he found himself fighting the same battles, but this time, with his own people. It was surely a discouraging realization.

I know from experience that the most difficult aspect of the ministry is dealing with sin in the camp. It's one thing to wage war against the devil. It's quite another to find that having defeated an enemy on the outside, you now have to deal with sin within the fellowship of God's people.

A Parting Shot

But Nehemiah again emerged victorious. The closing sentence of Nehemiah's book is the cry of a weary man who has fought a good fight: "Remember me, O my God, for good!"

That's the end of the story. It began with prayer, and it ends that way, too. It is a fitting way to finish the story of a truly great champion.

We certainly remember him for good. It is hard to view Nehemiah in any other light. He's a challenge to us all, to be all that we can be for God. If God could use a man like Nehemiah, He can also get a lot of mileage out of you. Or me. Or anyone who dares to rise up in His name and build in His strength and for His glory.

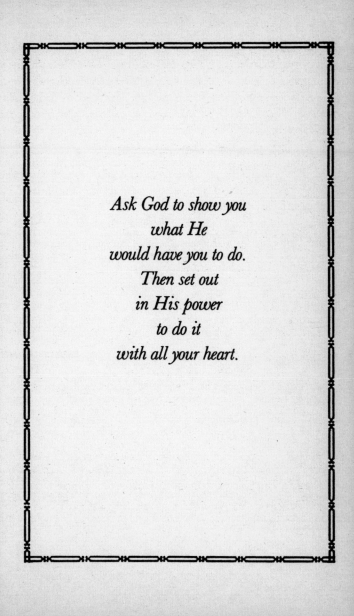

*Ask God to show you
what He
would have you to do.
Then set out
in His power
to do it
with all your heart.*

14

Righteousness Challenges a Permissive Society

*R*eflecting on the life and times of Nehemiah, we feel a strong sense of kinship with him. The society he lived in was much like ours. The wars he waged are still going on between the people of God and the Sanballats and Tobiahs. The same kinds of compromise he confronted in Jerusalem run rampant in the modern church.

We can learn a lot from this man. Lord, give us a double portion of his spirit!

Nehemiah stood out because he challenged the status quo. The status quo was wrong, and he wasn't afraid to say so. In fact, he shouted it aloud. His life and work were a rebuke to the permissiveness and compromise all around him. Yet people were drawn to his leadership. Why?

Because God always has His remnant. Even in our permissive society, there are, I know, thousands of knees that have not bowed to Baal. We needn't fear to speak out and challenge the ungodliness and corruption we live amidst. We needn't back down in silence just because the Sanballats and Tobiahs threaten and squawk. They always have. They always will.

The Modern Status Quo

Nehemiah speaks to our time like no other Old Testament character I know. As an untrained layman, he speaks to this age of lay leadership. As a great leader who organized and managed one of the most mammoth reconstruction projects in history, he speaks to modern man's fascination with management theory and leadership style. In fact, Nehemiah exemplifies the kinds of participatory leadership that advocates of modern management say work best.

On top of all that, the spiritual crises Nehemiah dealt with are exactly the same crises we're dealing with today: lack of conviction, half-hearted commitment, rampant compromise, and debilitating spiritual lethargy.

Like the Israelite nation of Nehemiah's day, the contemporary church is in a deplorable state of spiritual decay. High-pressure marketing tactics have replaced the leading of the Holy Spirit in motivating God's people for ministry. Decisions are made based on what's cost-effective rather than by seeking God's will. Money is raised by begging from God's people rather than by praying to God Himself. "Ministry" looks more like empire-building than genuine service to people. In short, the church has sold out to mammon.

Recent revelations about hidden sin in Christian leaders' lives have shocked even the secular world. The church has become known as a playground for hucksters and hypocrites. Its testimony to the world has been lost in the din of hype and controversy that the church itself has created. There are few remaining ministries that are committed more to biblical principles than to self-propagation, and in the world's eyes they get lumped in with everyone else.

The church's years of tolerance and compromise are finally demanding their dividends, and Christians stand to lose everything. Jesus said, "You are the salt of the earth; but if the salt loses its flavor, how shall it be seasoned? It is then good for nothing but to be thrown out and trampled under foot by men" (Matt. 5:13).

The salt has lost its flavor. Or, to change metaphors, the walls have crumbled around us. God's people are surrounded with the rubble of broken-down boulders, and the church is more vulnerable to the attacks of the enemy than it has ever been. We are in grave danger of being trodden under foot by men. It is time to begin to rebuild.

Never has Nehemiah's story been more relevant. Never have God's people been more exposed, more open to the enemy's onslaughts. Never have we been more in need of true champions.

The Time Is Right

God's people, I believe, are ready to rally around champions. Our age is ripe for revival. There are willing builders, ready to take up their tools and tackle the broken walls. If only true champions will step forward to lead the way! What about you?

You say, "I'm only a layperson."

So was Nehemiah.

"I'm just a working person."

So was Nehemiah.

"I don't have any training for it."

Neither did Nehemiah.

"But I'm busy with my job."

So was Nehemiah.

"Other people are better qualified."

That was true with Nehemiah.

You see, whatever excuses we think we have to keep from being champions for God, Nehemiah shatters those excuses. We are no different from him. He was no better than us. But in the hands of Jehovah God, to whom he had given himself completely, Nehemiah was ideal material for a great champion.

You can be a champion, too. Ask God to show you what He would have you to do, and then set out in His power to do it with all your heart. You will experience pain and suffering, like all true champions. You may be falsely accused and imprisoned, as Joseph was. You may have to spend some years in the desert, as Moses did. You may be persecuted and chased by evil men, as David was. You may be hated and even killed, as most of the disciples were.

But in the final analysis, whatever God chooses to permit you to endure, the blessings will far outweigh the pain and suffering.

Imagine if Nehemiah had been like most people. He

never would have petitioned the king to let him go to Jerusalem. He would have thought his life was too valuable to risk for the opportunity to rebuild some walls in a city he had never seen. He would have stayed in his comfortable job and hoped for someone else to do the dirty work.

And the world would have missed a great champion.

What Are You Willing to Do?

It's fine to pray that God will send someone to do a tough job. It's another thing entirely to be willing to be the one to step forward and risk it all. But that's the price of being a real champion.

Champions are a rare breed. They trust God while everyone else is asking for answers to questions. They step forward while everyone else prays for someone to volunteer. They see beyond the dangers, the risks, the obstacles, and the hardships. What they see instead is the power and glory of God.

Isaiah answered the call of God, "Here am I! Send me" (Isa. 6:8). That's the answer of every true champion. I hope that's your answer, and that you'll accept the challenge to be a champion for God. I don't know if He'll call you to build a wall or preach the gospel. I don't know what He'll give you to do.

But I *do* know that your world will never be the same.